The Merits And Rem. [...]

And The Baptism Of Infants

Saint Augustin

Kessinger Publishing's Rare Reprints

Thousands of Scarce and Hard-to-Find Books on These and other Subjects!

- Americana
- Ancient Mysteries
- Animals
- Anthropology
- Architecture
- Arts
- Astrology
- Bibliographies
- Biographies & Memoirs
- Body, Mind & Spirit
- Business & Investing
- Children & Young Adult
- Collectibles
- Comparative Religions
- Crafts & Hobbies
- Earth Sciences
- Education
- Ephemera
- Fiction
- Folklore
- Geography
- Health & Diet
- History
- Hobbies & Leisure
- Humor
- Illustrated Books
- Language & Culture
- Law
- Life Sciences
- Literature
- Medicine & Pharmacy
- Metaphysical
- Music
- Mystery & Crime
- Mythology
- Natural History
- Outdoor & Nature
- Philosophy
- Poetry
- Political Science
- Science
- Psychiatry & Psychology
- Reference
- Religion & Spiritualism
- Rhetoric
- Sacred Books
- Science Fiction
- Science & Technology
- Self-Help
- Social Sciences
- Symbolism
- Theatre & Drama
- Theology
- Travel & Explorations
- War & Military
- Women
- Yoga
- *Plus Much More!*

We kindly invite you to view our catalog list at:
http://www.kessinger.net

A TREATISE ON THE MERITS AND FORGIVENESS OF SINS, AND ON THE BAPTISM OF INFANTS,

BY AURELIUS AUGUSTIN, BISHOP OF HIPPO;

IN THREE BOOKS,

ADDRESSED TO MARCELLINUS, A.D. 412.

BOOK I.

IN WHICH HE REFUTES THOSE WHO MAINTAIN, THAT ADAM MUST HAVE DIED EVEN IF HE HAD NEVER SINNED; AND THAT NOTHING OF HIS SIN HAS BEEN TRANSMITTED TO HIS POSTERITY BY NATURAL DESCENT. HE ALSO SHOWS, THAT DEATH HAS NOT ACCRUED TO MAN BY ANY NECESSITY OF HIS NATURE, BUT AS THE PENALTY OF SIN; HE THEN PROCEEDS TO PROVE THAT IN ADAM'S SIN HIS ENTIRE OFFSPRING IS IMPLICATED, SHOWING THAT INFANTS ARE BAPTIZED FOR THE EXPRESS PURPOSE OF RECEIVING THE REMISSION OF ORIGINAL SIN.

CHAP. 1 [I.] — INTRODUCTORY, IN THE SHAPE OF AN INSCRIPTION TO HIS FRIEND MARCELLINUS.

HOWEVER absorbing and intense the anxieties and annoyances in the whirl and warmth of which we are engaged with sinful men [1] who forsake the law of God, — even though we may well ascribe these very evils to the fault of our own sins, — I am unwilling, and, to say the truth, unable, any longer to remain a debtor, my dearest Marcellinus,[2] to that zealous affection of yours, which only enhances my own grateful and pleasant estimate of yourself. I am under the impulse [of a twofold emotion]: on the one hand, there is that very love which makes us unchangeably one in the one hope of a change for the better; on the other hand, there is the fear of offending God in yourself, who has given you so earnest a desire, in gratifying which I shall be only serving Him who has given it to you. And so strongly has this impulse led and attracted me to solve, to the best of my humble ability, the questions which you have submitted to me in writing, that my mind has gradually admitted this inquiry to an importance transcending that of all others; [and it will now give me no rest] until I accomplish something which shall make it manifest that I have yielded, if not a sufficient, yet at any rate an obedient, compliance with your own kind wish and the desire of those to whom these questions are a source of anxiety.

CHAP. 2 [II.] — IF ADAM HAD NOT SINNED, HE WOULD NEVER HAVE DIED.

They who say that Adam was so formed that he would even without any demerit of sin have died, not as the penalty of sin, but from the necessity of his being, endeavour indeed to refer that passage in the law, which says: "On the day ye eat thereof ye shall surely die," [3] not to the death of

---

[1] This is probably an allusion to the Donatists, who were then fiercely assailing the Catholics; [and over the conference between whom and the Catholics, Marcellinus had presided the previous year (411). — W.]

[2] [Flavius Marcellinus, a "tribune and notary," a Christian man of high character and devout mind, who was much interested in theological discussions. He was appointed by Honorius to preside over the commission of inquiry into the disputes between the Catholics and Donatists in 411, and held the famous conference between the parties, that met in Carthage on the 1st, 3d, and 8th of June, 411. He discharged this whole business with singular patience, moderation, and good judgment; which appears to have cemented the intimate friendship between him and Augustin. Augustin's treatise on *The Spirit and Letter* is also addressed to him, and he undertook the *City of God* on his suggestion. See below, p. 80. — W.]

[3] Gen. ii. 17.

the body, but to that death of the soul which takes place in sin. It is the unbelievers who have died this death, to whom the Lord pointed when He said, "Let the dead bury their dead."[1] Now what will be their answer, when we read that God, when reproving and sentencing the first man after his sin, said to him, "Dust thou art, and unto dust shalt thou return?"[2] For it was not in respect of his soul that he was "dust," but clearly by reason of his body, and it was by the death of the self-same body that he was destined to "return to dust." Still, although it was by reason of his body that he was dust, and although he bare about the natural body in which he was created, he would, if he had not sinned, have been changed into a spiritual body, and would have passed into the incorruptible state, which is promised to the faithful and the saints, without the peril of death.[3] And for this issue we not only are conscious in ourselves of having an earnest desire, but we learn it from the apostle's intimation, when he says : "For in this we groan, longing to be clothed upon with our habitation which is from heaven ; if so be that being clothed we shall not be found naked. For we that are in this tabernacle do groan, being burdened ; not for that we would be unclothed, but clothed upon, that mortality may be swallowed up of life."[4] Therefore, if Adam had not sinned, he would not have been divested of his body, but would have been clothed upon with immortality and incorruption, that "mortality might have been swallowed up of life ; " that is, that he might have passed from the natural body into the spiritual body.

CHAP. 3 [III.] — IT IS ONE THING TO BE MORTAL, ANOTHER THING TO BE SUBJECT TO DEATH.

Nor was there any reason to fear that if he had happened to live on here longer in his natural body, he would have been oppressed with old age, and have gradually, by increasing age, arrived at death. For if God granted to the clothes and the shoes of the Israelites that "they waxed not old" during so many years,[5] what wonder if for obedience it had been by the power of the same [God] allowed to man, that although he had a natural and mortal body, he should have in it a certain condition, in which he might grow full of years without decrepitude, and, whenever God pleased, pass from mortality to immortality without the medium of death? For even as this very flesh of ours, which we now possess, is not therefore invulnerable, because it is not necessary that it should be wounded ; so also was his not therefore immortal, because there was no necessity for its dying. Such a condition, whilst

still in their natural and mortal body, I suppose, was granted even to those who were translated hence without death.[6] For Enoch and Elijah were not reduced to the decrepitude of old age by their long life. But yet I do not believe that they were then changed into that spiritual kind of body, such as is promised in the resurrection, and which the Lord was the first to receive ; only they probably do not need those aliments, which by their use minister refreshment to the body ; but ever since their translation they so live, as to enjoy such a sufficiency as was provided during the forty days in which Elijah lived on the cruse of water and the cake, without substantial food ;[7] or else, if there be any need of such sustenance, they are, it may be, sustained in Paradise in some such way as Adam was, before he brought on himself expulsion therefrom by sinning. And he, as I suppose, was supplied with sustenance against decay from the fruit of the various trees, and from the tree of life with security against old age.

CHAP. 4 [IV.] — EVEN BODILY DEATH IS FROM SIN.

But in addition to the passage where God in punishment said, " Dust thou art, unto dust shalt thou return,"[2] — a passage which I cannot understand how any one can apply except to the death of the body, — there are other testimonies likewise, from which it most fully appears that by reason of sin the human race has brought upon itself not spiritual death merely, but the death of the body also. The apostle says to the Romans : " But if Christ be in you, the body is dead because of sin, but the spirit is life because of righteousness. If therefore the Spirit of Him that raised up Jesus from the dead dwell in you, He that raised up Christ Jesus from the dead shall quicken also your mortal bodies by His Spirit that dwelleth in you."[8] I think that so clear and open a sentence as this only requires to be read, and not expounded. The body, says he, is dead, not because of earthly frailty, as being made of the dust of the ground, but because of sin; what more do we want? And he is most careful in his words : he does not say "is mortal," but "dead."

CHAP. 5 [V.] — THE WORDS, MORTALE (CAPABLE OF DYING), MORTUUM (DEAD), AND MORITURUS (DESTINED TO DIE).

Now previous to the change into the incorruptible state which is promised in the resurrection of the saints, the body could be mortal (capable of dying), although not destined to die (moriturus) ; just as our body in its present state can, so to speak, be capable of sickness, although not destined to be sick. For whose is the flesh which is

---

[1] Matt. viii. 22; Luke ix. 60.
[2] Gen. iii. 19.
[3] 1 Cor. xv. 52, 53.
[4] 2 Cor. v. 2–4.
[5] Deut. xxix. 5.

[6] Gen. v. 24; 2 Kings ii. 11.
[7] 1 Kings xix. 8.
[8] Rom. viii. 10, 11.

incapable of sickness, even if from some accident it die before it ever is sick? In like manner was man's body then mortal; and this mortality was to have been superseded by an eternal incorruption, if man had persevered in righteousness, that is to say, obedience: but even what was mortal (*mortale*) was not made dead (*mortuum*), except on account of sin. For the change which is to come in at the resurrection is, in truth, not only not to have death incidental to it, which has happened through sin, but neither is it to have mortality, [or the very possibility of death,] which the natural body had before it sinned. He does not say: "He that raised up Christ Jesus from the dead shall quicken also your *dead* bodies" (although he had previously said, "the body is dead"[1]); but his words are: "He shall quicken also your *mortal* bodies;"[2] so that they are not only no longer dead, but no longer mortal [or capable of dying], since the natural is raised spiritual, and this mortal body shall put on immortality, and mortality shall be swallowed up in life.[3]

CHAP. 6 [VI.] — HOW IT IS THAT THE BODY IS DEAD BECAUSE OF SIN.

One wonders that anything is required clearer than the proof we have given. But we must perhaps be content to hear this clear illustration gainsaid by the contention, that we must understand "the dead body" here[1] in the sense of the passage where it is said, "Mortify your members which are upon the earth."[4] But it is *because of righteousness* and not because of sin that the body is in this sense mortified; for it is to do the works of righteousness that we mortify our bodies which are upon the earth. Or if they suppose that the phrase, "because of sin," is added, not that we should understand "because sin has been committed," but "in order that sin may not be committed" — as if it were said, "The body indeed is dead, in order to prevent the commission of sin:" what then does he mean in the next clause by adding the words, "because of righteousness," to the statement, "The spirit is life?"[1] For it would have been enough simply to have adjoined "the spirit is life," to have secured that we should supply here too, "in order to prevent the commission of sin;" so that we should thus understand the two propositions to point to one thing — that both "the body is dead," and "the spirit is life," for the one common purpose of "preventing the commission of sin." So likewise if he had merely' meant to say, "because of righteousness," in the sense of "for the purpose of doing righteousness," the two clauses might possibly be referred to this one purpose — to the effect, that both "the body is dead," and "the spirit is life," "for the purpose of doing righteousness." But as the passage actually stands, it declares that "the body is dead because of sin," and "the spirit is life because of righteousness," attributing different merits to different things — the demerit of sin to the death of the body, and the merit of righteousness to the life of the spirit. Wherefore if, as no one can doubt, "the spirit is life because of righteousness," that is, as the desert, of righteousness; how ought we, or can we, understand by the statement, "The body is dead because of sin," anything else than that the body is dead as the desert of sin, unless indeed we try to pervert or wrest the plainest sense of Scripture to our own arbitrary will? But besides this, additional light is afforded by the words which follow. For it is with limitation to the present time, when he says, that on the one hand "the body is dead because of sin," since, whilst the body is unrenovated by the resurrection, there remains in it the desert of sin, that is, the necessity of dying; and on the other hand, that "the spirit is life because of righteousness," since, notwithstanding the fact of our being still burdened with "the body of this death,"[5] we have already by the renewal which is begun in our inner man, new aspirations[6] after the righteousness of faith. Yet, lest man in his ignorance should fail to entertain hope of the resurrection of the body, he says that the very body which he had just declared to be "dead because of sin" in this world, will in the next world be made alive "because of righteousness," — and that not only in such a way as to become alive from the dead, but immortal from its mortality.

CHAP. 7 [VII.] — THE LIFE OF THE BODY THE OBJECT OF HOPE, THE LIFE OF THE SPIRIT BEING A PRELUDE TO IT.

Although I am much afraid that so clear a matter may rather be obscured by exposition, I must yet request your attention to the luminous statement of the apostle. "But if Christ," says he, "be in you, the body indeed is dead because of sin, but the spirit is life because of righteousness."[1] Now this is said, that men may not suppose that they derive no benefit, or but scant benefit, from the grace of Christ, seeing that they must needs die in the body. For they are bound to remember that, although their body still bears that desert of sin, which is irrevocably bound to the condition of death, yet their spirit has already begun to live because of the righteousness of faith, although it had actually become extinct by the death, as it were, of unbelief. No small gift, therefore, he says, must you suppose to have been conferred

---

[1] Rom. viii. 10.
[2] Rom. viii. 11.
[3] 1 Cor. xv. 44, 53, 55.
[4] Col. iii. 5.

[5] Rom. vii. 24.
[6] Respiramus.

upon you, by the circumstance that Christ is in you; inasmuch as in the body, which is dead because of sin, your spirit is even now alive because of righteousness; so that therefore you should not despair of the life even of your body. "For if the Spirit of Him that raised up Christ from the dead dwell in you, He that raised up Christ from the dead shall quicken also your mortal bodies by His Spirit that dwelleth in you." [1] How is it that fumes of controversy still darken so clear a light? The apostle distinctly tells you, that although the body is dead because of sin within you, yet even your mortal bodies shall be made alive because of righteousness, because of which even now your spirit is life, — the whole of which process is to be perfected by the grace of Christ, that is, by His Spirit dwelling in you: and men still contradict! He goes on to tell us how it comes to pass that life converts death into itself by mortifying it. "Therefore, brethren," says he, "we are debtors, not to the flesh, to live after the flesh; for if ye live after the flesh, ye shall die; but if ye through the spirit do mortify the deeds of the flesh, ye shall live." [2] What else does this mean but this: If ye live according to death, ye shall wholly die; but if by living according to life ye mortify death, ye shall wholly live?

CHAP. 8 [VIII.] — BODILY DEATH FROM ADAM'S SIN.

When to the like purport he says: "By man came death, by man also the resurrection of the dead," [3] in what other sense can the passage be understood than of the death of the body; for having in view the mention of this, he proceeded to speak of the resurrection of the body, and affirmed it in a most earnest and solemn discourse? In these words, addressed to the Corinthians: "By man came death, and by man came also the resurrection of the dead; for as in Adam all die, even so in Christ shall all be made alive," [4] — what other meaning is indeed conveyed than in the verse in which he says to the Romans, "By one man sin entered into the world, and death by sin?" [5] Now they will have it, that the death here meant is the death, not of the body, but of the soul, on the pretence that another thing is spoken of to the Corinthians, where they are quite unable to understand the death of the soul, because the subject there treated is the resurrection of the body, which is the antithesis of the death of the body. The reason, moreover, why only death is here mentioned as caused by man, and not sin also, is because the point of the discourse is not about righteousness, which is the

antithesis of sin, but about the resurrection of the body, which is contrasted with the death of the body.

CHAP. 9 [IX.] — SIN PASSES ON TO ALL MEN BY NATURAL DESCENT, AND NOT MERELY BY IMITATION.

You tell me in your letter, that they endeavour to twist into some new sense the passage of the apostle, in which he says: "By one man sin entered into the world, and death by sin;" [5] yet you have not informed me what they suppose to be the meaning of these words. But so far as I have discovered from others, they think that the death which is here mentioned is not the death of the body, which they will not allow Adam to have deserved by his sin, but that of the soul, which takes place in actual sin; and that this actual sin has not been transmitted from the first man to other persons by natural descent, but by imitation. Hence, likewise, they refuse to believe that in infants original sin is remitted through baptism, for they contend that no such original sin exists at all in people by their birth. But if the apostle had wished to assert that sin entered into the world, not by natural descent, but by imitation, he would have mentioned as the first offender, not Adam indeed, but the devil, of whom it is written, [6] that "he sinneth from the beginning;" of whom also we read in the Book of Wisdom: "Nevertheless through the devil's envy death entered into the world." [7] Now, forasmuch as this death came upon men from the devil, not because they were propagated by him, but because they imitated his example, it is immediately added: "And they that do hold of his side do imitate him." [8] Accordingly, the apostle, when mentioning sin and death together, which had passed by natural descent from one upon all men, set him down as the introducer thereof from whom the propagation of the human race took its beginning.

CHAP. 10. — THE ANALOGY OF GRACE.

No doubt all they imitate Adam who by disobedience transgress the commandment of God; but he is one thing as an example to those who sin because they choose; and another thing as the progenitor of all who are born with sin. All His saints, also, imitate Christ in the pursuit of righteousness; whence the same apostle, whom we have already quoted, says: "Be ye imitators of me, as I am also of Christ." [9] But besides this imitation, His grace works within us our illumination and justification, by that operation concerning which the same preacher of His [name] says: "Neither is he that planteth anything, nor he that watereth, but God that giveth the

---

[1] Rom. viii. 11.
[2] Rom. viii. 12, 13.
[3] 1 Cor. xv. 21.
[4] 1 Cor. xv. 21, 22.
[5] Rom. v. 12.

[6] 1 John iii. 8.
[7] Wisd. ii. 24.
[8] Ver. 25.
[9] 1 Cor. xi. 1.

increase." [1] For by this grace He engrafts into His body even baptized infants, who certainly have not yet become able to imitate any one. As therefore He, in whom all are made alive, besides offering Himself as an example of righteousness to those who imitate Him, gives also to those who believe on Him the hidden grace of His Spirit, which He secretly infuses even into infants ; so likewise he, in whom all die, besides being an example for imitation to those who wilfully transgress the commandment of the Lord, depraved also in his own person all who come of his stock by the hidden corruption of his own carnal concupiscence. It is entirely on this account, and for no other reason, that the apostle says : "By one man sin entered into the world, and death by sin, and so passed upon all men ; in which all have sinned." [2] Now if *I* were to say this, they would raise an objection, and loudly insist that I was incorrect both in expression and sense ; for they would perceive no sense in these words when spoken by an ordinary man, except that sense which they refuse to see in the apostle. Since, however, these are the words of him to whose authority and doctrine they submit, they charge us with slowness of understanding, while they endeavour to wrest to some unintelligible sense words which were written in a clear and obvious purport. "By one man," says he, "sin entered into the world, and death by sin." This indicates propagation, not imitation ; for if imitation were meant, he would have said, "By the devil." But as no one doubts, he refers to that first man who is called Adam : "And so," says he, "it passed upon all men."

CHAP. 11 [X.] — DISTINCTION BETWEEN ACTUAL AND ORIGINAL SIN. [3]

Again, in the clause which follows, "In which all have sinned," how cautiously, rightly, and unambiguously is the statement expressed ! For if you understand that sin to be meant which by one man entered into the world, "In which [sin] all have sinned," it is surely clear enough, that the sins which are peculiar to every man, which they themselves commit and which belong simply to them, mean one thing; and that the one sin, in and by which all have sinned, means another thing; since all were that one man. If, however, it be not the sin, but that one man that is understood, "In which [one man] all have sinned," what again can be plainer than even this clear statement? We read, indeed, of those being justified in Christ who believe in Him, by reason of the secret communion and inspiration of that spiritual grace which makes every one who cleaves to the Lord "one spirit" with

Him,[4] although His saints also imitate His example ; can I find, however, any similar statement made of those who have imitated His saints ? Can any man be said to be justified in Paul or in Peter, or in any one whatever of those excellent men whose authority stands high among the people of God? We are no doubt said to be blessed in Abraham, according to the passage in which it was said to him, "In thee shall all nations be blessed" [5] — for Christ's sake, who is his seed according to the flesh ; which is still more clearly expressed in the parallel passage : "In thy seed shall all nations be blessed." I do not believe that any one can find it anywhere stated in the Holy Scriptures, that a man has ever sinned or still sins "in the devil," although all wicked and impious men "imitate" him. The apostle, however, has declared concerning the first man, that "in him all have sinned ;" [2] and yet there is still a contest about the propagation of sin, and men oppose to it I know not what nebulous theory of "imitation." [6]

CHAP. 12. — THE LAW COULD NOT TAKE AWAY SIN.

Observe also what follows. Having said, "In which all have sinned," he at once added, "For until the law, sin was in the world." [7] This means that sin could not be taken away even by the law, which entered that sin might the more abound,[8] whether it be the law of nature, under which every man when arrived at years of discretion only proceeds to add his own sins to original sin, or that very law which Moses gave to the people. "For if there had been a law given which could have given life, verily righteousness should have been by the law. But the Scripture hath concluded all under sin, that the promise by faith in Jesus Christ might be given to them that believe.[9] But sin is not imputed where there is no law." [7] Now what means the phrase "*is not imputed*," but "*is ignored*," or "*is not reckoned as sin?*" Although the Lord God does not Himself regard it as if it had never been, since it is written : "As many as have sinned without law shall also perish without law." [10]

CHAP. 13 [XI.] — MEANING OF THE APOSTLE'S PHRASE "THE REIGN OF DEATH."

"Nevertheless," says he, "death reigned from Adam even unto Moses," [11] — that is to say, from

---

[1] 1 Cor. iii. 7.
[2] Rom. v. 12.
[3] See below, Book iii. c. vii.; also in the *De Nuptiis*, c. v.; also *Epist* 186. and *Serm* 165.
[4] 1 Cor. vi. 17.
[5] Gal iii. 8: comp. Gen. xii. 3, xviii 18, xxii. 18.
[6] This was the Pelagian term, expressive of their dogma that original sin stands in the following [or "imitation"] of Adam, instead of being the fault and corruption of the nature of every man who is naturally engendered of Adam's offspring; which doctrine is expressed by Augustin's word, *propagatio*, "propagation."
[7] Rom. v. 13.
[8] Rom. v. 20.
[9] Gal. iii. 21, 22.
[10] Rom. ii. 12.
[11] Rom. v. 14.

the first man even to the very law which was promulged by the divine authority, because even it was unable to abolish the reign of death. Now death must be understood "to reign," whenever the guilt of sin [1] so dominates in men that it prevents their attainment of that eternal life which is the only true life, and drags them down even to the second death which is penally eternal. This reign of death is only destroyed in any man by the Saviour's grace, which wrought even in the saints of the olden time, all of whom, though previous to the coming of Christ in the flesh, yet lived in relation to His assisting grace, not to the letter of the law, which only knew how to command, but not to help them. In the Old Testament, indeed, that was hidden (conformably to the perfectly just dispensation of the times) which is now revealed in the New Testament. Therefore " death reigned from Adam unto Moses," in all who were not assisted by the grace of Christ, that in them the kingdom of death might be destroyed, " even in those who had not sinned after the similitude of Adam's transgression," [2] that is, who had not yet sinned of their own individual will, as Adam did, but had drawn from him original sin, " who is the figure of him that was to come," [2] because in him was constituted the form of condemnation to his future progeny, who should spring from him by natural descent; so that from one all men were born to a condemnation, from which there is no deliverance but in the Saviour's grace. I am quite aware, indeed, that several Latin copies of the Scriptures read the passage thus : " Death reigned from Adam to Moses over them who have sinned after the similitude of Adam's transgression ; " [3] but even this version is referred by those who so read it to the very same purport, for they understood those who have sinned in him to have sinned after the similitude of Adam's transgression ; so that they are created in his likeness, not only as men born of a man, but as sinners born of a sinner, dying ones of a dying one, and condemned ones to a condemned one. However, the Greek copies from which the Latin version was made, have all, without exception or nearly so, the reading which I first adduced.

CHAP. 14.—SUPERABUNDANCE OF GRACE.

" But," says he, " not as the offence so also is the free gift. For if, through the offence of one, many be dead, much more the grace of God, and the gift by grace, which is by One Man, Jesus Christ, hath abounded unto many." [4]

[1] Reatus peccati.
[2] Rom. v. 14.
[3] Comp. Epist. 157, n. 19. [Some few Greek copies have come down to us (e.g. 67**) which omit the "not," but no Latin copy (unless d* be an exception), although other Latin writers (e.g. Ambrosiaster) testify to their former existence. — W.]
[4] Rom. v. 15.

Not *many more*, that is, many more men, for there are not more persons justified than condemned ; but it runs, *much more hath abounded ;* inasmuch as, while Adam produced sinners from his one sin, Christ has by His grace procured free forgiveness even for the sins which men have of their own accord added by actual transgression to the original sin in which they were born. This he states more clearly still in the sequel.

CHAP. 15 [XII.] — THE ONE SIN COMMON TO ALL MEN.

But observe more attentively what he says, that " through the offence of one, many are dead." For why should it be on account of the sin of one, and not rather on account of their own sins, if this passage is to be understood of *imitation*, and not of *propagation ?* [5] But mark what follows : " And not as it was by one that sinned, so is the gift ; for the judgment was by one to condemnation, but the grace is of many offences unto justification." [6] Now let them tell us, where there is room in these words for *imitation*. " By one," says he, " to condemnation." By one what except one sin ? This, indeed, he clearly implies in the words which he adds : " But the grace is of many offences unto justification." Why, indeed, is the judgment from one offence to condemnation, while the grace is from many offences to justification? If original sin is a nullity, would it not follow, that not only grace withdraws men from many offences to justification, but judgment leads them to condemnation from many offences likewise ? For assuredly grace does not condone many offences, without judgment in like manner having many offences to condemn. Else, if men are involved in condemnation because of one offence, on the ground that all the offences which are condemned were committed in imitation of that one offence ; there is the same reason why men should also be regarded as withdrawn from one offence unto justification, inasmuch as all the offences which are remitted to the justified were committed in imitation of that one offence. But this most certainly was not the apostle's meaning, when he said : "The judgment, indeed, was from *one* offence unto condemnation, but the grace was from *many* offences unto justification." We on our side, indeed, can understand the apostle, and see that judgment is predicated of one offence unto condemnation entirely on the ground that, even if there were in men nothing but original sin, it would be sufficient for their condemnation. For however much heavier will be their condemnation who have added their own sins to

[5] See note to last word of ch. 11.
[6] Rom. v. 16.

the original offence (and it will be the more severe in individual cases, in proportion to the sins of individuals) ; still, even that sin alone which was originally derived unto men not only excludes from the kingdom of God, which infants are unable to enter (as they themselves allow), unless they have received the grace of Christ before they die, but also alienates from salvation and everlasting life, which cannot be anything else than the kingdom of God, to which fellowship with Christ alone introduces us.

CHAP. 16 [XIII.] — HOW DEATH IS BY ONE AND LIFE BY ONE.

And from this we gather that we have derived from Adam, in whom we all have sinned, not all our actual sins, but only original sin ; whereas from Christ, in whom we are all justified, we obtain the remission not merely of that original sin, but of the rest of our sins also, which we have added. Hence it runs : " Not as by the one that sinned, so also is the free gift." For the judgment, certainly, from one sin, if it is not remitted — and that the original sin — is capable of drawing us into condemnation ; whilst grace conducts us to justification from the remission of many sins, — that is to say, not simply from the original sin, but from all others also whatsoever.

CHAP. 17. — WHOM SINNERS IMITATE.

" For if by one man's offence death reigned by one ; much more they which receive abundance of grace and of righteousness shall reign in life by one, even Jesus Christ." [1] Why did death reign on account of the sin of one, unless it was that men were bound by the chain of death in that one man in whom all men sinned, even though they added no sins of their own? Otherwise it was not on account of the sin of one that death reigned through one ; rather it was on account of the manifold offences of many, [operating] through each individual sinner. For if the reason why men have died for the transgression of another be, that they have imitated him by following him as their predecessor in transgression, it must even result, and *that* " much more," that that one died on account of the transgression of another, whom the devil so preceded in transgression as himself to persuade him to commit the transgression. Adam, however, used no influence to persuade his followers ; and the many who are said to have imitated him have, in fact, either not heard of his existence at all or of his having committed any such sin as is ascribed to him, or altogether disbelieve it. How much more correctly, therefore, as I have already remarked,[2] would the apostle have set

forth the devil as the author, from which " one " he would say that sin and death had passed upon all, if he had in this passage meant to speak, not of propagation, but of imitation? For there is much stronger reason for saying that Adam is an imitator of the devil, since he had in *him* an actual instigator to sin ; if one may be an imitator even of him who has never used any such persuasion, or of whom he is absolutely ignorant. But what is implied in the clause, " They which receive abundance of grace and righteousness," but that the grace of remission is given not only to that sin in which all have sinned, but to those offences likewise which men have actually committed besides ; and that on these [men] so great a righteousness is freely bestowed, that, although Adam gave way to him who persuaded him to sin, they do not yield even to the coercion of the same tempter? Again, what mean the words, " Much more shall they reign in life," when the fact is, that the reign of death drags many more down to eternal punishment, unless we understand those to be really mentioned in both clauses, who pass from Adam to Christ, in other words, from death to life ; because in the life eternal they shall reign without end, and thus exceed the reign of death which has prevailed within them only temporarily and with a termination?

CHAP. 18. — ONLY CHRIST JUSTIFIES.

" Therefore as by the offence of one upon all men to condemnation, even so by the justification of One upon all men unto justification of life." [3] This " offence of one," if we are bent on " imitation," can only be the devil's offence. Since, however, it is manifestly spoken in reference to Adam and not the devil, it follows that we have no other alternative than to understand the principle of natural propagation, and not that of imitation, to be here implied. [XIV.] Now when he says in reference to Christ, " By the *justification* of one," he has more expressly stated our doctrine than if he were to say, " By the *righteousness* of one ; " inasmuch as he mentions that justification whereby Christ justifies the ungodly, and which he did not propose as an object of imitation, for He alone is capable of effecting this. Now it was quite competent for the apostle to say, and to say rightly : " Be ye imitators of me, as I also am of Christ ; " [4] but he could never say : Be ye justified by me, as I also am by Christ ; — since there may be, and indeed actually are and have been, many who were righteous and worthy of imitation ; but no one is righteous and a justifier but Christ alone. Whence it is said : " To the man that believeth on him that justifieth the ungodly, his faith is counted

[1] Rom. v. 17.
[2] See above, ch. 9.
[3] Rom. v. 18.
[4] 1 Cor. iv. 16; xi. 1.

for righteousness." [1] Now if any man had it in his power confidently to declare, " I justify you," it would necessarily follow that he could also say, " Believe in me." But it has never been in the power of any of the saints of God to say this except the Saint of saints,[2] who said : " Ye believe in God, believe also in me ; " [3] so that, inasmuch as it is He that justifies the ungodly, to the man who believes in him that justifieth the ungodly his faith is imputed for righteousness.

CHAP. 19 [XV.] — SIN IS FROM NATURAL DESCENT, AS RIGHTEOUSNESS IS FROM REGENERATION ; HOW " ALL " ARE SINNERS THROUGH ADAM, AND " ALL " ARE JUST THROUGH CHRIST.

Now if it is imitation only that makes men sinners through Adam, why does not imitation likewise alone make men righteous through Christ ? " For," he says, " as by the offence of one upon all men to condemnation ; even so by the justification of one upon all men unto justification of life." [4] [On the theory of imitation], then, the " *one* " and the " *one*," here, must not be regarded as Adam and Christ, but Adam and Abel. For although many sinners have preceded us in the time of this present life, and have been imitated in their sin by those who have sinned at a later date, yet they will have it, that only Adam is mentioned as he in whom all have sinned by imitation, since he was the first of men who sinned. And on the same principle, Abel ought certainly to have been mentioned, as he " in which one " all likewise are justified by imitation, inasmuch as he was himself the first man who lived justly. If, however, it be thought necessary to take into the account some critical period having relation to the beginning of the New Testament, and Christ be taken as the leader of the righteous and the object of their imitation, then Judas, who betrayed Him, ought to be set down as the leader of the class of sinners. Moreover, if Christ alone is He in whom all men are justified, on the ground that it is not simply the imitation of His example which makes men just, but His grace which regenerates men by the Spirit, then also Adam is the only one in whom all have sinned, on the ground that it is not the mere following of his evil example that makes men sinners, but the penalty which generates through the flesh. Hence the terms " *all men* " and " *all men*." For not they who are generated through Adam are actually the very same as those who are regenerated through Christ ; but yet the language of the apostle is strictly correct, because as none partakes of carnal generation except through Adam, so no one shares in the spiritual except through Christ.

For if any could be generated in the flesh, yet not by Adam ; and if in like manner any could be generated in the Spirit, and not by Christ ; clearly " *all* " could not be spoken of either in the one class or in the other. But these " *all* " [5] the apostle afterwards describes as " *many ;* " [6] for obviously, under certain circumstances, the " all " may be but a few. The carnal generation, however, embraces " *many*," and the spiritual generation also includes " *many ;* " although the " many " of the spiritual are less numerous than the " many " of the carnal. But as the one embraces *all* men whatever, so the other includes *all* righteous men ; because as in the former case none can be a man without the carnal generation, so in the other class no one can be a righteous man without the spiritual generation ; in both instances, therefore, there are " many : " " For as by the disobedience of one man *many* were made sinners, so by the obedience of one shall *many* be made righteous." [7]

CHAP. 20. — ORIGINAL SIN ALONE IS CONTRACTED BY NATURAL BIRTH.

" Moreover the law entered, that the offence might abound." [8] This addition to original sin men now made of their own wilfulness, not through Adam ; but even this is done away and remedied by Christ, because "where sin abounded, grace did much more abound ; that as sin hath reigned unto death " [9] — even that sin which men have not derived from Adam, but have added of their own will — " even so might grace reign through righteousness unto eternal life." [9] There is, however, other righteousness apart from Christ, as there are other sins apart from Adam. Therefore, after saying, " As sin hath reigned unto death," he did not add in the same clause " *by one*," or " *by Adam*," because he had already spoken of that sin which was abounding when the law entered, and which, of course, was not original sin, but the sin of man's own wilful commission. But after he has said : " Even so might grace also reign through righteousness unto eternal life," he at once adds, " through Jesus Christ our Lord ; " [9] because, whilst by the generation of the flesh only that sin is contracted which is original ; yet by the regeneration of the Spirit there is effected the remission not of original sin only, but also of the sins of man's own voluntary and actual commission.

CHAP. 21 [XVI.] — UNBAPTIZED INFANTS DAMNED, BUT MOST LIGHTLY ; [10] THE PENALTY OF ADAM'S SIN, THE GRACE OF HIS BODY LOST.

It may therefore be correctly affirmed, that

---

[1] Rom. iv. 5.
[2] Sanctus sanctorum.
[3] John xiv. 1.
[4] Rom. v. 18.
[5] The word is " *all* " in ver. 18.
[6] See ver. 19.
[7] Rom. v. 19.
[8] Rom. v. 20.
[9] Rom. v. 21.
[10] See Augustin's *Enchirid.* c. 93, and *Contra Julianum*, v. 11.

such infants as quit the body without being baptized will be involved in the mildest condemnation of all. That person, therefore, greatly deceives both himself and others, who teaches that they will not be involved in condemnation ; whereas the apostle says : " Judgment from one offence to condemnation," [1] and again a little after : " By the offence of one upon all persons to condemnation." [2]   When, indeed, Adam sinned by not obeying God, then his body — although it was a natural and mortal body — lost the grace whereby it used in every part of it to be obedient to the soul. Then there arose in men affections common to the brutes which are productive of shame, and which made man ashamed of his own nakedness.[3]   Then also, by a certain disease which was conceived in men from a suddenly injected and pestilential corruption, it was brought about that they lost that stability of life in which they were created, and, by reason of the mutations which they experienced in the stages of life, issued at last in death. However many were the years they lived in their subsequent life, yet they began to die on the day when they received the law of death, because they kept verging towards old age. For that possesses not even a moment's stability, but glides away without intermission, which by constant change perceptibly advances to an end which does not produce perfection, but utter exhaustion.   Thus, then, was fulfilled what God had spoken : " In the day that ye eat thereof, ye shall surely die." [4]   As a consequence, then, of this disobedience of the flesh and this law of sin and death, whoever is born of the flesh has need of spiritual regeneration — not only that he may reach the kingdom of God, but also that he may be freed from the damnation of sin. Hence men are on the one hand born in the flesh liable to sin and death from the first Adam, and on the other hand born again in baptism associated with the righteousness and eternal life of the second Adam ; even as it is written in the book of Ecclesiasticus : " Of the woman came the beginning of sin, and through her we all die." [5]   Now whether it be said of the woman or of Adam, both statements pertain to the first man ; since (as we know) the woman is of the man, and the two are one flesh.   Whence also it is written : " And they twain shall be one flesh ; wherefore," the Lord says, " they are no more twain, but one flesh." [6]

CHAP. 22 [XVII.] — TO INFANTS PERSONAL SIN IS NOT TO BE ATTRIBUTED.

They, therefore, who say that the reason why infants are baptized, is, that they may have the remission of the sin which they have themselves committed in their life, not what they have derived from Adam, may be refuted without much difficulty.   For whenever these persons shall have reflected within themselves a little, uninfluenced by any polemical spirit, on the absurdity of their statement, how unworthy it is, in fact, of serious discussion, they will at once change their opinion.   But if they will not do this, we shall not so completely despair of men's common sense, as to have any fears that they will induce others to adopt their views.   They are themselves driven to adopt their opinion, if I am not mistaken, by their prejudice for some other theory ; and it is because they feel themselves obliged to allow that sins are remitted to the baptized, and are unwilling to allow that the sin was derived from Adam which they admit to be remitted to infants, that they have been obliged to charge infancy itself with actual sin ; as if by bringing this charge against infancy a man could become the more secure himself, when accused and unable to answer his assailant !   However, let us, as I suggested, pass by such opponents as these ; indeed, we require neither words nor quotations of Scripture to prove the sinlessness of infants, so far as their conduct in life is concerned ; this life they spend, such is the recency of their birth, within their very selves, since it escapes the cognizance of human perception, which has no data or support whereon to sustain any controversy on the subject.

CHAP. 23 [XVIII.] — HE REFUTES THOSE WHO ALLEGE THAT INFANTS ARE BAPTIZED NOT FOR THE REMISSION OF SINS, BUT FOR THE OBTAINING OF THE KINGDOM OF HEAVEN.[7]

But those persons raise a question, and appear to adduce an argument deserving of consideration and discussion, who say that new-born infants receive baptism not for the remission of sin, but that, since their procreation is not spiritual, they may be created in Christ, and become partakers of the kingdom of heaven, and by the same means children and heirs of God, and joint-heirs with Christ.   And yet, when you ask them, whether those that are not baptized, and are not made joint-heirs with Christ and partakers of the kingdom of heaven, have at any rate the blessing of eternal life in the resurrection of the dead, they are extremely perplexed, and find no way out of their difficulty.   For what Christian is there who would allow it to be said, that any one could attain to eternal salvation without being born again in Christ, — [a result] which He meant to be effected through baptism, at the very time when such a sacrament

---

[1] Rom. v. 16.
[2] Ver. 18.
[3] Gen. iii. 10.
[4] Gen. ii. 17.
[5] Ecclus. xxv. 24.
[6] Matt. xix. 5, 6.

[7] See below, c. 26; also *De Peccato orig.* c. 19–24; also *Serm.* 294.

was purposely instituted for regenerating in the hope of eternal salvation? Whence the apostle says: "Not by works of righteousness which we have done, but according to His mercy He saved us by the laver[1] of regeneration."[2] This salvation, however, he says, consists in hope, while we live here below, where he says, "For we are saved by hope: but hope that is seen is not hope; for what a man seeth, why doth he yet hope for? But if we hope for that we see not, then do we with patience wait for it."[3] Who then could be so bold as to affirm, that without the regeneration of which the apostle speaks, infants could attain to eternal salvation, as if Christ died not for them? For "Christ died for the ungodly."[4] As for them, however, who (as is manifest) never did an ungodly act in all their own life, if also they are not bound by any bond of sin in their original nature, how did He die for them, who died for *the ungodly?* If they were hurt by no malady of original sin, how is it they are carried to the Physician Christ, for the express purpose of receiving the sacrament of eternal salvation, by the pious anxiety of those who run to Him? Why rather is it not said to them in the Church: Take hence these innocents: "they that are whole need not a physician, but they that are sick;" — Christ "came not to call the righteous, but sinners?"[5] There never has been heard, there never is heard, there never will be heard in the Church, such a fiction concerning Christ.

CHAP. 24 [XIX.] — INFANTS SAVED AS SINNERS.

And let no one suppose that infants ought to be brought to baptism, on the ground that, as they are not sinners, so they are not righteous; how then do some remind us that the Lord commends this tender age as meritorious; saying, "Suffer the little children to come unto me, and forbid them not, for of such is the kingdom of heaven?"[6] For if this ["of such"] is not said because of likeness in humility (since humility makes [us] children), but because of the laudable life of children, then of course infants must be righteous persons; otherwise, it could not be correctly said, "Of such is the kingdom of heaven," for heaven can only belong to the righteous. But perhaps, after all, it is not a right opinion of the meaning of the Lord's words, to make Him commend the life of infants when He says, "Of such is the kingdom of heaven;" inasmuch as *that* may be their true sense, which makes Christ adduce the tender age of infancy as a likeness of humility. Even so, however,

perhaps we must revert to the tenet which I mentioned just now, that infants ought to be baptized, because, although they are not sinners, they are yet not righteous. But when He had said: "I came not to call the righteous," as if responding to this, Whom, then, didst Thou come to call? immediately He goes on to say: " — but sinners to repentance." Therefore it follows, that, however righteous they may be, if also they are not sinners, He came not to call them, who said of Himself: "I came not to call the righteous, but sinners." They therefore seem, not vainly only, but even wickedly to rush to the baptism of Him who does not invite them, — an opinion which God forbid that we should entertain. He calls them, then, as a Physician who is not needed for those that are whole, but for those that are sick; and who came not to call the righteous, but sinners to repentance. Now, inasmuch as infants are not held bound by any sins of their own actual life, it is the guilt of original sin which is healed in them by the grace of Him who saves them by the laver of regeneration.

CHAP. 25. — INFANTS ARE DESCRIBED AS BELIEVERS AND AS PENITENTS. SINS ALONE SEPARATE BETWEEN GOD AND MEN.

Some one will say: How then are mere infants called to repentance? How can such as they repent of anything? The answer to this is: If they must not be called penitents because they have not the sense of repenting, neither must they be called believers, because they likewise have not the sense of believing. But if they are rightly called believers,[7] because they in a certain sense profess faith by the words of their parents, why are they not also held to be before that penitents when they are shown to renounce the devil and this world by the profession again of the same parents? The whole of this is done in hope, in the strength of the sacrament and of the divine grace which the Lord has bestowed upon the Church. But yet who knows not that the baptized infant fails to be benefited from what he received as a little child, if on coming to years of reason he fails to believe and to abstain from unlawful desires? If, however, the infant departs from the present life after he has received baptism, the guilt in which he was involved by original sin being done away, he shall be made perfect in that light of truth, which, remaining unchangeable for evermore, illumines the justified in the presence of their Creator. For sins alone separate between men and God; and these are done away by Christ's grace, through whom, as Mediator, we are reconciled, when He justifies the ungodly.

---

[1] Lavacrum.
[2] Tit. iii. 5.
[3] Rom. viii. 24, 25.
[4] Rom. v. 6.
[5] Luke v. 31, 32.
Matt. xix. 14.

---

[7] See below, c. 26 and 40; also Book iii. c. 2; also *Epist.* 98, and *Serm.* 294.

CHAP. 26 [XX.] — NO ONE, EXCEPT HE BE BAP-
TIZED, RIGHTLY COMES TO THE TABLE OF THE
LORD.

Now they take alarm from the statement of the
Lord, when He says, "Except a man be born
again, he cannot see the kingdom of God;"[1]
because in His own explanation of the passage
He affirms, "Except a man be born of water and
of the Spirit, he cannot enter into the kingdom
of God."[2] And so they try to ascribe to unbaptized infants, by the merit of their innocence, the
gift of salvation and eternal life, but at the same
time, owing to their being unbaptized, to exclude
them from the kingdom of heaven. But how
novel and astonishing is such an assumption, as
if there could possibly be salvation and eternal
life without heirship with Christ, without the kingdom of heaven! Of course they have their refuge,
whither to escape and hide themselves, because
the Lord does not say, Except a man be born of
water and of the Spirit, he cannot have life, but —
"he cannot enter into the kingdom of God." If
indeed He had said the other, there could have
risen not a moment's doubt. Well, then, let us
remove the doubt; let us now listen to the Lord,
and not to men's notions and conjectures; let us,
I say, hear what the Lord says — not indeed concerning the sacrament of the laver, but concerning the sacrament of His own holy table, to
which none but a baptized person has a right
to approach: "Except ye eat my flesh and
drink my blood, ye shall have no life in you."[3]
What do we want more? What answer to this
can be adduced, unless it be by that obstinacy
which ever resists the constancy of manifest
truth?

CHAP. 27. — INFANTS MUST FEED ON CHRIST.

Will, however, any man be so bold as to say
that this statement has no relation to infants, and
that they can have life in them without partaking of His body and blood — on the ground
that He does not say, Except *one* eat, but "Except *ye* eat;" as if He were addressing those
who were able to hear and to understand, which
of course infants cannot do? But he who says
this is inattentive; because, unless *all* are embraced in the statement, that without the body
and the blood of the Son of man men cannot
have life, it is to no purpose that even the elder
age is solicitous of it. For if you attend to the
mere words, and not to the meaning, of the Lord
as He speaks, this passage may very well seem
to have been spoken merely to the people whom
He happened at the moment to be addressing;
because He does not say, Except *one* eat; but
Except *ye* eat. What also becomes of the state-

ment which He makes in the same context on
this very point: "The bread that I will give is
my flesh, for the life of the world?"[4] For, it
is according to this statement, that we find that
that sacrament pertains also to us, who were not
in existence at the time the Lord spoke these
words; for we cannot possibly say that we do
not belong to "the world," for the life of which
Christ gave His flesh. Who indeed can doubt
that in the term *world* all persons are indicated
who enter the world by being born? For, as
He says in another passage, "The children of
this world beget and are begotten."[5] From all
this it follows, that even for the life of *infants*
was His flesh given, which He gave for the life
of the world; and that even they will not have
life if they eat not the flesh of the Son of man.

CHAP. 28. — BAPTIZED INFANTS, OF THE FAITH-
FUL; UNBAPTIZED, OF THE LOST.

Hence also that other statement: "The
Father loveth the Son, and hath given all things
into His hand. He that believeth on the Son
hath everlasting life; while he that believeth not
the Son shall not see life, but the wrath of God
abideth on him."[6] Now in which of these
classes must we place infants — amongst those
who believe on the Son, or amongst those who
believe not the Son? In neither, say some, because, as they are not yet able to believe, so
must they not be deemed unbelievers. This,
however, the rule of the Church does not indicate, for it joins baptized infants to the number
of the faithful. Now if they who are baptized
are, by virtue of the excellence and administra-
tion of so great a sacrament, nevertheless reckoned in the number of the faithful, although by
their own heart and mouth they do not literally
perform what appertains to the action of faith
and confession; surely they who have lacked
the sacrament must be classed amongst those
who do not believe on the Son, and therefore,
if they shall depart this life without this grace,
they will have to encounter what is written concerning such — they shall not have life, but the
wrath of God abideth on them. Whence could
this result to those who clearly have no sins of
their own, if they are not held to be obnoxious
to original sin?

CHAP. 29 [XXI.] — IT IS AN INSCRUTABLE MYS-
TERY WHY SOME ARE SAVED, AND OTHERS NOT.

Now there is much significance in that He does
not say, "The wrath of God *shall come* upon him,"
but "*abideth* on him." For from this wrath (in
which we are all involved under sin, and of which
the apostle says, "For we too were once by nature

---

[1] John iii. 3.
[2] Ver. 5.
[3] John vi. 53.

[4] John vi. 51.
[5] Generant et generantur; Luke xx. 34.
[6] John iii. 35, 36.

the children of wrath, even as others"[1]) nothing delivers us but the grace of God, through Jesus Christ our Lord. The reason why this grace comes upon one man and not on another may be hidden, but it cannot be unjust. For "is there unrighteousness with God? God forbid."[2] But we must first bend our necks to the authority of the Holy Scriptures, in order that we may each arrive at knowledge and understanding through faith. For it is not said in vain, "Thy judgments are a great deep."[3] The profundity of this "deep" the apostle, as if with a feeling of dread, notices in that exclamation: "O the depth of the riches both of the wisdom and the knowledge of God!" He had indeed previously pointed out the meaning of this marvellous depth, when he said: "For God hath concluded them all in unbelief, that He might have mercy upon all."[4] Then struck, as it were, with a horrible fear of this deep: "O the depth of the riches both of the wisdom and the knowledge of God! how unsearchable are His judgments, and His ways past finding out! For who hath known the mind of the Lord? or who hath been His counsellor? or who hath first given to Him, and it shall be recompensed unto him again? For of Him, and through Him, and in Him, are all things: to whom be glory for ever. Amen."[5] How utterly insignificant, then, is our faculty for discussing the justice of God's judgments, and for the consideration of His gratuitous grace, which, as men have no prevenient merits for deserving it, cannot be partial or unrighteous, and which does not disturb us when it is bestowed upon unworthy men, as much as when it is denied to those who are equally unworthy!

CHAP. 30. — WHY ONE IS BAPTIZED AND ANOTHER NOT, NOT OTHERWISE INSCRUTABLE.

Now those very persons, who think it unjust that infants which depart this life without the grace of Christ should be deprived not only of the kingdom of God, into which they themselves admit that none but such as are regenerated through baptism can enter, but also of eternal life and salvation, — when they ask how it can be just that one man should be freed from original sin and another not, although the condition of both of them is the same, might answer their own question, in accordance with their own opinion of how it can be so frequently just and right that one should have baptism administered to him whereby to enter into the kingdom of God, and another not be so favoured, although the case of both is alike. For if the question disturbs him, why, of the two persons, who are

both equally sinners by nature, the one is loosed from that bond, on whom baptism is conferred, and the other is not released, on whom such grace is not bestowed; why is he not similarly disturbed by the fact that of two persons, innocent by nature, one receives baptism, whereby he is able to enter into the kingdom of God, and the other does not receive it, so that he is incapable of approaching the kingdom of God? Now in both cases one recurs to the apostle's outburst of wonder, "O the depth of the riches!" Again, let me be informed, why out of the body of baptized infants themselves, one is taken away, so that his understanding undergoes no change from a wicked life,[6] and the other survives, destined to become an impious man? Suppose both were carried off, would not both enter the kingdom of heaven? And yet there is no unrighteousness with God.[2] How is it that no one is moved, no one is driven to the expression of wonder amidst such depths, by the circumstance that some children are vexed by the unclean spirit, while others experience no such pollution, and others again, as Jeremiah, are sanctified even in their mother's womb;[7] whereas all men, if there is original sin, are equally guilty; or else equally innocent if there is original sin? Whence this great diversity, except in the fact that God's judgments are unsearchable, and His ways past finding out?

CHAP. 31 [XXII.] — HE REFUTES THOSE WHO SUPPOSE THAT SOULS, ON ACCOUNT OF SINS COMMITTED IN ANOTHER STATE, ARE THRUST INTO BODIES SUITED TO THEIR MERITS, IN WHICH THEY ARE MORE OR LESS TORMENTED.

Perhaps, however, the now exploded and rejected opinion must be resumed, that souls which once sinned in their heavenly abode, descend by stages and degrees to bodies suited to their deserts, and, as a penalty for their previous life, are more or less tormented by corporeal chastisements. To this opinion Holy Scripture indeed presents a most manifest contradiction; for when recommending divine grace, it says: "For the children being not yet born, neither having done any good or evil, that the purpose of God according to election might stand, not of works, but of Him that calleth, it was said, The elder shall serve the younger."[8] And yet they who entertain such an opinion are actually unable to escape the perplexities of this question, but, embarrassed and straitened by them, are compelled to exclaim like others, "O the depth!" For whence does it come to pass that a person shall from his earliest boyhood show greater moderation, mental excellence, and temperance, and shall to a great extent conquer

---

[1] Eph. ii. 3.
[2] Rom. ix. 14.
[3] Ps. xxxvi. 6.
[4] Rom. xi. 32.
[5] Rom. xi. 33-36.

[6] Wisdom iv. 11.
[7] Jer. i. 5.
[8] Rom. ix. 11, 12.

lust, shall hate avarice, detest luxury, and rise to a greater eminence and aptitude in the other virtues, and yet live in such a place as to be unable to hear the grace of Christ preached?— for "how shall they call on Him in whom they have not believed? or how shall they believe in Him of whom they have not heard? and how shall they hear without a preacher?"[1] While another man, although of a slow mind, addicted to lust, and covered with disgrace and crime, shall be so directed as to hear, and believe, and be baptized, and be taken away, — or, if permitted to remain longer here, lead the rest of his life in a manner that shall bring him praise? Now where did these two persons acquire such diverse deserts, — I do not say, that the one should believe and the other not believe, for that is a matter for a man's own will; but that the one should hear in order to believe, and that the other should not hear, for this is not within man's power? Where, I say, did they acquire diverse deserts? If they had indeed passed any part of their life in heaven, so as to be thrust down, or to sink down, to this world, and to tenant such bodily receptacles as are congruous to their own former life, then of course that man ought to be supposed to have led the better life previous to his present mortal body, who did not much deserve to be burdened with it, so as both to have a good disposition, and to be importuned by milder desires which he could easily overcome; and yet he did not deserve to have that grace preached to him whereby alone he could be delivered from the ruin of the second death. Whereas the other, who was hampered with a grosser body, as a penalty — so they suppose — for worse deserts, and was accordingly possessed of obtuser affections, whilst he was in the violent ardour of his lust succumbing to the snares of the flesh, and by his wicked life aggravating his former sins, which had brought him to such a pass, by a still more abandoned course of earthly pleasures, — either heard upon the cross, "To-day shalt thou be with me in paradise,"[2] or else joined himself to some apostle, by whose preaching he became a changed man, and was saved by the washing of regeneration, — so that where sin once abounded, grace did much more abound. I am at a loss to know what answer they can give to this who wish to maintain God's righteousness by human conjectures, and, knowing nothing of the depths of grace, have woven webs of improbable fable.

CHAP. 32. — THE CASE OF CERTAIN IDIOTS AND SIMPLETONS.

Now a good deal may be said of men's strange vocations, — either such as we have read about,

or have experienced ourselves, — which go to overthrow the opinion of those persons who think that, previous to the possession of their bodies, men's souls passed through certain lives peculiar to themselves, in which they must come to this, and experience in the present life either good or evil, according to the difference of their individual deserts. My anxiety, however, to bring this work to an end does not permit me to dwell longer on these topics. But on one point, which among many I have found to be a very strange one, I will not be silent. If we follow those persons who suppose that souls are oppressed with earthly bodies in a greater or a less degree of grossness, according to the deserts of the life which had been passed in celestial bodies previous to the assumption of the present one, who would not affirm that those had sinned previous to this life with an especial amount of enormity, who deserve so to lose all mental light, that they are born with faculties akin to brute animals, — who are (I will not say most slow in intellect, for this is very commonly said of others also, but) so silly as to make a show of their fatuity for the amusement of clever people, even with idiotic gestures,[3] and whom the vulgar call, by a name derived from the Greek, *Moriones?*[4] And yet there was once a certain person of this class, who was so Christian, that although he was patient to the degree of strange folly with any amount of injury to himself, he was yet so impatient of any insult to the name of Christ, or, in his own person, to the religion with which he was imbued, that he could never refrain, whenever his gay and clever audience proceeded to blaspheme the sacred name, as they sometimes would in order to provoke his patience, from pelting them with stones; and on these occasions he would show no favour even to persons of rank. Well, now, such persons are predestinated and brought into being, as I suppose, in order that those who are able should understand that God's grace and the Spirit, "which bloweth where it listeth,"[5] does not pass over any kind of capacity in the sons of mercy, nor in like manner does it pass over any kind of capacity in the children of Gehenna, so that "he that glorieth, let him glory in the Lord."[6] They, however, who affirm that souls severally receive different earthly bodies, more or less gross according to the merits of their former life, and that their abilities as men vary according to the self-same merits, so that some minds are sharper and others more obtuse, and that the grace of God is also dispensed for

---

[1] Rom. x. 14.
[2] Luke xxiii. 43.

[3] We here follow the reading *cerriti;* other readings are, — *curati* (with studied folly), *cirrati* (with effeminate foppery), and *citrati* (decking themselves with *citrus* leaves).
[4] That is, "fools," from the Greek μωρός.
[5] John iii. 8.
[6] 1 Cor. i. 31.

the liberation of men from their sins according to the deserts of their former existence : — what will they have to say about this man? How will they be able to attribute to him a previous life of so disgraceful a character that he deserved to be born an idiot, and at the same time of so highly meritorious a character as to entitle him to a preference in the award of the grace of Christ over many men of the acutest intellect?

CHAP. 33. — CHRIST IS THE SAVIOUR AND RE-DEEMER EVEN OF INFANTS.

Let us therefore give in and yield our assent to the authority of Holy Scripture, which knows not how either to be deceived or to deceive ; and as we do not believe that men as yet unborn have done any good or evil for raising a difference in their moral deserts, so let us by no means doubt that all men are under sin, which came into the world by one man and has passed through unto all men ; and from which nothing frees us but the grace of God through our Lord Jesus Christ. [XXIII.] His remedial advent is needed by those that are sick, not by the whole : for He came not to call the righteous, but sinners ; and into His kingdom shall enter no one that is not born again of water and the Spirit ; nor shall any one attain salvation and eternal life except in His kingdom, — since the man who believes not in the Son, and eats not His flesh, shall not have life, but the wrath of God remains upon him. Now from this sin, from this sickness, from this wrath of God (of which by nature they are children who have original sin, even if they have none of their own on account of their youth), none delivers them, except the Lamb of God, who takes away the sins of the world ;[1] except the Physician, who came not for the sake of the sound, but of the sick ; except the Saviour, concerning whom it was said to the human race : "Unto you there is born this day a Saviour ;"[2] except the Redeemer, by whose blood our debt is blotted out. For who would dare to say that Christ is not the Saviour and Redeemer of infants? But from what does He save them, if there is no malady of original sin within them? From what does He redeem them, if through their origin from the first man they are not sold under sin? Let there be then no eternal salvation promised to infants out of our own opinion, without Christ's baptism ; for none is promised in that Holy Scripture which is to be preferred to all human authority and opinion.

CHAP. 34 [XXIV.] — BAPTISM IS CALLED SALVA-TION, AND THE EUCHARIST, LIFE, BY THE CHRISTIANS OF CARTHAGE.

The Christians of Carthage have an excellent name for the sacraments, when they say that baptism is nothing else than "salvation," and the sacrament of the body of Christ nothing else than "life." Whence, however, was this derived, but from that primitive, as I suppose, and apostolic tradition, by which the Churches of Christ maintain it to be an inherent principle, that without baptism and partaking of the supper of the Lord it is impossible for any man to attain either to the kingdom of God or to salvation and everlasting life? So much also does Scripture testify, according to the words which we already quoted. For wherein does their opinion, who designate baptism by the term *salvation*, differ from what is written : " He *saved us* by the washing of regeneration?"[3] or from Peter's statement : " The like figure whereunto even baptism doth also *now save us?*"[4] And what else do they say who call the sacrament of the Lord's Supper *life*, than that which is written : " I am the *living* bread which came down from heaven ; "[5] and " The bread that I shall give is my flesh, for *the life* of the world ; "[5] and " Except ye eat the flesh of the Son of man, and drink His blood, ye shall have no life in you?"[6] If, therefore, as so many and such divine witnesses agree, neither salvation nor eternal life can be hoped for by any man without baptism and the Lord's body and blood, it is vain to promise these blessings to infants without them. Moreover, if it be only sins that separate man from salvation and eternal life, there is nothing else in infants which these sacraments can be the means of removing, but the guilt of sin, — respecting which guilty nature it is written, that "no one is clean, not even if his life be only that of a day."[7] Whence also that exclamation of the Psalmist : " Behold, I was shapen in iniquity ; and in sin did my mother conceive me ! "[8] This is either said in the person of our common humanity, or if of himself only David speaks, it does not imply that he was born of fornication, but in lawful wedlock. We therefore ought not to doubt that even for infants yet to be baptized was that precious blood shed, which previous to its actual effusion was so given, and applied in the sacrament, that it was said, " This is my blood, which shall be shed for many for the remission of sins."[9] Now they who will not allow that they are under sin, deny that there is any liberation. For what is there that men are liberated from, if they are held to be bound by no bondage of sin?

[1] John. i. 29.
[2] Luke ii. 11.
[3] Tit. iii. 5.
[4] 1 Pet. iii. 21
[5] John vi. 51.
[6] John vi. 53.
[7] Job xiv. 4.
[8] Ps. li. 5.
[9] Matt. xxvi. 28.

CHAP. 35. — UNLESS INFANTS ARE BAPTIZED, THEY REMAIN IN DARKNESS.

" I am come," says Christ, " a light into the world, that whosoever believeth on me should not abide in darkness." [1] Now what does this passage show us, but that every person is in darkness who does not believe on Him, and that it is by believing on Him that he escapes from this permanent state of darkness? What do we understand by the *darkness* but sin? And whatever else it may embrace in its meaning, at any rate he who believes not in Christ will " abide in darkness," — which, of course, is a penal state, not, as the darkness of the night, necessary for the refreshment of living beings. [xxv.] So that infants, unless they pass into the number of believers through the sacrament which was divinely instituted for this purpose, will undoubtedly remain in this darkness.

CHAP. 36. — INFANTS NOT ENLIGHTENED AS SOON AS THEY ARE BORN.

Some, however, understand that as soon as children are born they are enlightened ; and they derive this opinion from the passage : " That was the true Light, which lighteth every one that cometh into the world." [2] Well, if this be the case, it is quite astonishing how it can be that those who are thus enlightened by the only-begotten Son, who was in the beginning the Word with God, and [Himself] God, are not admitted into the kingdom of God, nor are heirs of God and joint-heirs with Christ. For that such an inheritance is not bestowed upon them except through baptism, even they who hold the opinion in question do acknowledge. Then, again, if they are (though already illuminated) thus unfit for entrance into the kingdom of God, they at all events ought gladly to receive the baptism, by which they are fitted for it ; but, strange to say, we see how reluctant infants are to submit to baptism, resisting even with strong crying. And this ignorance of theirs we think lightly of at their time of life, so that we fully administer the sacraments, which we know to be serviceable to them, even although they struggle against them. And why, too, does the apostle say, " Be not children in understanding," [3] if their minds have been already enlightened with that true Light, which is the Word of God?

CHAP. 37. — HOW GOD ENLIGHTENS EVERY PERSON.

That statement, therefore, which occurs in the gospel, " That was the true Light, which lighteth every one that cometh into the world," [2] has this meaning, that no man is illuminated except with that Light of the truth, which is God ; so that no person must think that he is enlightened by him whom he listens to as a learner, although that instructor happen to be — I will not say, any great man — but even an angel himself. For the word of truth is applied to man externally by the ministry of a bodily voice, but yet " neither is he that planteth any thing, neither he that watereth ; but God that giveth the increase." [4] Man indeed hears the speaker, be he man or angel, but in order that he may perceive and know that what is said is true, his mind is internally besprinkled with that light which remains for ever, and which shines even in darkness. But just as the sun is not seen by the blind, though they are clothed as it were with its rays, so is the light of truth not understood by the darkness of folly.

CHAP. 38. — WHAT " LIGHTETH " MEANS.

But why, after saying, " which lighteth every man," should he add, " that cometh into the world," [2] — the clause which has suggested the opinion that He enlightens the minds of newly-born babes while the birth of their bodies from their mother's womb is still a recent thing? The words, no doubt, are so placed in the Greek, that they may be understood to express that the light itself " cometh into the world." [5] If, nevertheless, the clause must be taken as expressing the man who cometh into this world, I suppose that it is either a simple phrase, like many others one finds in the Scriptures, which may be removed without impairing the general sense ; or else, if it is to be regarded as a distinctive addition, it was perhaps inserted in order to distinguish spiritual illumination from that bodily one which enlightens the eyes of the flesh either by means of the luminaries of the sky, or by the lights of ordinary fire. So that he mentioned the inner man as coming into the world, because the outward man is of a corporeal nature, just as this world itself; as if he said, " Which lighteth every man that cometh into the body," in accordance with that which is written : " I obtained a good spirit, and I came in a body undefiled." [6] Or again, the passage, " Which lighteth every one that cometh into the world," — if it was added for the sake of expressing some distinction, — might perhaps mean : Which lighteth every inner man, because the inner man, when he becomes truly wise, is enlightened only by Him who is the true Light. Or, once more, if the intention was to designate reason herself, which causes the human soul to be called rational (and this reason, although as yet quiet and as it were asleep, for all that lies hidden in

---

[1] John xii. 46.
[2] John i. 9.
[3] 1 Cor. xiv. 20.

[4] 1 Cor. iii. 7.
[5] Ὁ [scil. τὸ φῶς] φωτίζει πάντα ἄνθρωπον ἐρχόμενον εἰς τὸν κόσμον.
[6] Wisd. viii. 19, 20.

infants, innate and, so to speak, implanted), by the term *illumination*, as if it were the creation of an inner eye, then it cannot be denied that it is made when the soul is created ; and there is no absurdity in supposing this to take place when the human being comes into the world. But yet, although his eye is now created, he himself must needs remain in darkness, if he does not believe in Him who said : " I am come a a Light into the world, that whosoever believeth on me should not abide in darkness." [1] And that this takes place in the case of infants, through the sacrament of baptism, is not doubted by mother Church, which uses for them the heart and mouth of a mother, that they may be imbued with the sacred mysteries, seeing that they cannot as yet with their own heart " believe unto righteousness," nor with their own mouth make " confession unto salvation." [2] There is not indeed a man among the faithful, who would hesitate to call such infants *believers* merely from the circumstance that such a designation is derived from the act of believing ; for although incapable of such an act themselves, yet others are sponsors for them in the sacraments.

CHAP. 39 [XXVI.] — THE CONCLUSION DRAWN, THAT ALL ARE INVOLVED IN ORIGINAL SIN.

It would be tedious, were we fully to discuss, at similar length, every testimony bearing on the question. I suppose it will be the more convenient course simply to collect the passages together which may turn up, or such as shall seem sufficient for manifesting the truth, that the Lord Jesus Christ came in the flesh, and, in the form of a servant, became obedient even to the death of the cross,[3] for no·other reason than, by this dispensation of His most merciful grace, to give life to all those to whom, as engrafted members of His body, He becomes Head for laying hold upon the kingdom of heaven : to save, free, redeem, and enlighten them, — who had aforetime been involved in the death, infirmities, servitude, captivity, and darkness of sin, under the dominion of the devil, the author of sin : and thus to become the Mediator between God and man, by whom (after the enmity of our ungodly condition had been terminated by His gracious help) we might be reconciled to God unto eternal life, having been rescued from the eternal death which threatened such as us. When this shall have been made clear by more than sufficient evidence, it will follow that those persons cannot be concerned with that dispensation of Christ which is executed by His humiliation, who have no need of life, and salvation,

and deliverance, and redemption, and illumination. And inasmuch as to this belongs baptism, in which we are buried with Christ, in order to be incorporated into Him as His members (that is, as those who believe in Him) : it of course follows that baptism is unnecessary for them, who have no need of the benefit of that forgiveness and reconciliation which is acquired through a Mediator. Now, seeing that they admit the necessity of baptizing infants, — finding themselves unable to contravene that authority of the universal Church, which has been unquestionably handed down by the Lord and His apostles, — they cannot avoid the further concession, that infants require the same benefits of the Mediator, in order that, being washed by the sacrament and charity of the faithful, and thereby incorporated into the body of Christ, which is the Church, they may be reconciled to God, and so live in Him, and be saved, and delivered, and redeemed, and enlightened. But from what, if not from death, and the vices, and guilt, and thraldom, and darkness of sin? And, inasmuch as they do not commit any sin in the tender age of infancy by their actual transgression, original sin only is left.

CHAP. 40 [XXVII.] — A COLLECTION OF SCRIPTURE TESTIMONIES. FROM THE GOSPELS.

This reasoning will carry more weight, after I have collected the mass of Scripture testimonies which I have undertaken to adduce. We have already quoted : " I came not to call the righteous, but sinners." [4] To the same purport [the Lord] says, on entering the home of Zaccheus : " To-day is salvation come to this house, forsomuch as he also is a son of Abraham ; for the Son of man is come to seek and to save that which was lost." [5] The same truth is declared in the parable of the lost sheep and the ninety and nine which were left until the missing one was sought and found ; [6] as it is also in the parable of the lost one among the ten silver coins.[7] Whence, as He said, " it behoved that repentance and remission of sins should be preached in His name among all nations, beginning at Jerusalem." [8] Mark likewise, at the end of his Gospel, tells us how that the Lord said : " Go ye into all the world, and preach the gospel to every creature. He that believeth, and is baptized, shall be saved ; but he that believeth not shall be damned." [9] Now, who can be unaware that, in the case of infants, being baptized is to believe, and not being baptized is not to believe? From the Gospel of John we have already ad-

[1] John xii. 46.
[2] Rom. x. 10.
[3] Phil. ii 8.

[4] Luke v. 32.
[5] Luke xix. 9, 10.
[6] Luke xv. 4.
[7] Luke xv. 8.
[8] Luke xxiv. 46, 47.
[9] Mark xvi. 15, 16.

duced some passages. However, I must also request your attention to the following : John Baptist says of Christ, " Behold the Lamb of God, Behold Him which taketh away the sin of the world ; " [1] and He too says of Himself, " My sheep hear my voice, and I know them, and they follow me : and I give unto them eternal life ; and they shall never perish." [2] Now, inasmuch as infants are only able to become His sheep by baptism, it must needs come to pass that they perish if they are not baptized, because they will not have that eternal life which He gives to His sheep. So in another passage He says : " I am the way, the truth, and the life ; no man cometh unto the Father, but by me." [3]

CHAP. 41. — FROM THE FIRST EPISTLE OF PETER.

See with what earnestness the apostles declare this doctrine, when they received it. Peter, in his first Epistle, says : " Blessed be the God and Father of our Lord Jesus Christ, according to His abundant mercy, who hath regenerated us unto the hope of eternal life, by the resurrection of Jesus Christ, to an inheritance immortal, and undefiled, flourishing, reserved in heaven for you, who are kept by the power of God through faith unto salvation, ready to be revealed in the last time." [4] And a little afterwards he adds : " May ye be found unto the praise and honour of Jesus Christ : of whom ye were ignorant ; but in whom ye believe, though now ye see Him not ; and in whom also ye shall rejoice, when ye shall see Him, with joy unspeakable and full of glory : receiving the end of your faith, even the salvation of your souls." [5] Again, in another place he says : " But ye are a chosen generation, a royal priesthood, a holy nation, a peculiar people ; that ye should show forth the praises of Him who hath called you out of darkness into His marvellous light." [6] Once more he says : " Christ hath once suffered for our sins, the just for the unjust, that He might bring us to God : " [7] and, after mentioning the fact of eight persons having been saved in Noah's ark, he adds : " And by the like figure baptism saveth you." [8] Now infants are strangers to this salvation and light, and will remain in perdition and darkness, unless they are joined to the people of God by adoption, holding to Christ who suffered the just for the unjust, to bring them unto God.

CHAP. 42. — FROM THE FIRST EPISTLE OF JOHN.

Moreover, from John's Epistle I meet with the following words, which seem indispensable to the solution of this question : " But if," says he, " we walk in the light, as He is in the light, we have fellowship one with another, and the blood of Jesus Christ His Son cleanseth us from all sin." [9] To the like import he says, in another place : " If we receive the witness of men, the witness of God is greater : for this is the witness of God, which is greater because He hath testified of His Son. He that believeth on the Son of God hath the witness in himself : he that believeth not God hath made Him a liar ; because he believed not in the testimony that God testified of His Son. And this is the testimony, that God hath given to us eternal life ; and this life is in His Son. He that hath the Son hath life ; and he that hath not the Son of God hath not life." [10] It seems, then, that it is not only the kingdom of heaven, but life also, which infants are not to have, if they have not the Son, whom they can only have by His baptism. So again he says : " For this cause the Son of God was manifested, that He might destroy the works of the devil." [11] Therefore infants will have no interest in the manifestation of the Son of God, if He do not in them destroy the works of the devil.

CHAP. 43. — FROM THE EPISTLE TO THE ROMANS.

Let me now request your attention to the testimony of the Apostle Paul on this subject. And quotations from him may of course be made more abundantly, because he wrote more epistles, and because it fell to him to recommend the grace of God with especial earnestness, in opposition to those who gloried in their works, and who, ignorant of God's righteousness, and wishing to establish their own, submitted not to the righteousness of God. [12] In his Epistle to the Romans he writes : " The righteousness of God is upon all them that believe ; for there is no difference ; since all have sinned, and come short of the glory of God ; being justified freely by His grace, through the redemption that is in Christ Jesus ; whom God hath set forth as a propitiation through faith in His blood, to declare His righteousness for the remission [13] of sins that are past, through the forbearance of God ; to declare, I say, at this time His righteousness ; that He might be just, and the justifier of him which believeth in Jesus." [14] Then in another passage he says : " To him that worketh is the reward not reckoned of grace, but of debt. But to him that worketh not, but believeth on Him that justifieth the ungodly, his faith is counted for righteousness. Even as David also describeth

---

[1] John i. 29.
[2] John x. 27, 28.
[3] John xiv. 6.
[4] 1 Pet. i. 3-5.
[5] 1 Pet. i 7-9.
[6] 1 Pet. ii. 9.
[7] 1 Pet. iii. 18.
[8] 1 Pet. iii. 21.

[9] 1 John i. 7.
[10] 1 John v. 9-12.
[11] 1 John iii. 8.
[12] Rom. x. 3.
[13] [This is the reading of the Vulgate, as well as of the Greek : but Augustin, following an Old Latin reading, actually has *propositum*, instead of *remissionem*. — W.]
[14] Rom. iii. 22-26.

the blessedness of the man, unto whom God imputeth righteousness without works, saying, Blessed are they whose iniquities are forgiven, and whose sins are covered. Blessed is the man to whom the Lord imputeth no sin." [1] And then after no long interval he observes: "Now, it was not written for his sake alone, that it was imputed to him; but for us also, to whom it shall be imputed, if we believe on Him that raised up Jesus Christ our Lord from the dead; who was delivered for our offences, and was raised again for our justification." [2] Then a little after he writes: "For when we were yet without strength, in due time Christ died for the ungodly." [3] In another passage he says: "We know that the law is spiritual; but I am carnal, sold under sin. For that which I do I know not: for what I would, that I do not; but what I hate, that I do. If then I do that which I would not, I consent unto the law that it is good. Now then, it is no more I that do it, but sin that dwelleth in me. For I know that in me (that is, in my flesh) dwelleth no good thing; for to will is present with me; but how to perform that which is good I find not. For the good that I would I do not; but the evil which I would not, that I do. Now if I do that I would not, it is no more I that do it, but sin that dwelleth in me. I find then a law, that, when I would do good, evil is present with me. For I delight in the law of God after the inward man: but I see another law in my members warring against the law of my mind, and bringing me into captivity to the law of sin which is in my members. O wretched man that I am! who shall deliver me from the body of this death? The grace of God, through Jesus Christ our Lord." [4] Let them, who can, say that men are not born in the body of this death, that so they may be able to affirm that they have no need of God's grace through Jesus Christ in order to be delivered from the body of this death. Therefore he adds, a few verses afterwards: "For what the law could not do, in that it was weak through the flesh, God, sending His own Son in the likeness of sinful flesh, and for sin, condemned sin in the flesh." [5] Let them say, who dare, that Christ must have been born in the likeness of sinful flesh, if we were not born in sinful flesh.

CHAP. 44. — FROM THE EPISTLES TO THE CORINTHIANS.

Likewise to the Corinthians he says: "For I delivered to you first of all that which I also received, how that Christ died for our sins according to the Scriptures." [6] Again, in his Second Epistle to these Corinthians: "For the love of Christ constraineth us; because we thus judge, that if One died for all, then all died: and for all did Christ die, that they which live should no longer live unto themselves, but unto Him which died for them, and rose again. Wherefore, henceforth know we no man after the flesh; yea, though we have known Christ after the flesh, yet from henceforth know we Him so no more. Therefore if any man be in Christ, he is a new creature; old things are passed away; behold, all things are become new. And all things are of God, who hath reconciled us to Himself by Jesus Christ, and hath given unto us the ministry of reconciliation. To what effect? That God was in Christ, reconciling the world unto Himself, not imputing their trespasses unto them, and putting on us the ministry of reconciliation. Now then are we ambassadors for Christ, as though God did beseech you by us; we pray you in Christ's stead, to be reconciled to God. For He hath made Him to be sin for us, who knew no sin; that we might become the righteousness of God in Him. [7] We then, as workers together with Him, beseech you also that ye receive not the grace of God in vain. (For He saith, I have heard thee in an acceptable time, and in the day of salvation have I succoured thee: behold, now is the acceptable time; behold, now is the day of salvation.)" [8] Now, if infants are not embraced within this reconciliation and salvation, who wants them for the baptism of Christ? But if they are embraced, then are they reckoned as among the dead for whom He died; nor can they be possibly reconciled and saved by Him, unless He remit and impute not unto them their sins.

CHAP. 45. — FROM THE EPISTLE TO THE GALATIANS.

Likewise to the Galatians the apostle writes: "Grace be to you, and peace, from God the Father, and from our Lord Jesus Christ, who gave Himself for our sins, that He might deliver us from this present evil world." [9] While in another passage he says to them: "The law was added because of transgressions, until the seed should come to whom the promise was made; and it was ordained by angels in the hand of a mediator. Now a mediator belongs not to one party; but God is one. Is the law then against the promises of God? God forbid: for if there had been a law given which could have given life, verily righteousness should have been by the law. But the scripture hath concluded all under sin, that the promise by faith of Jesus Christ might be given to them that believe." [10]

---

[1] Rom. iv. 4-8.
[2] Rom. iv. 23-25.
[3] Rom. v. 6.
[4] Rom. vii. 14-25.
[5] Rom. viii. 3.
[6] 1 Cor. xv. 3.

[7] 2 Cor. v. 14-21.
[8] 2 Cor. vi. 1, 2.
[9] Gal. i. 3, 4.
[10] Gal. iii. 19-22.

CHAP. 46. — FROM THE EPISTLE TO THE
EPHESIANS.

To the Ephesians he addresses words of the
same import : " And you when ye were dead
in trespasses and sins ; wherein in time past ye
walked according to the course of this world,
according to the prince of the power of the air,
the spirit of him that now worketh in the children of disobedience ; among whom also we all
had our conversation in times past in the lusts
of our flesh, fulfilling the desires of the flesh
and of the mind ; and were by nature the children of wrath, even as others.   But God, who is
rich in mercy, for His great love wherewith He
loved us, even when we were dead in sins, hath
quickened us together with Christ ; by whose
grace ye are saved." [1]   Again, a little afterwards,
he says : " By grace are ye saved through faith ;
and that not of yourselves : it is the gift of God :
not of works, lest any man should boast.   For
we are His workmanship, created in Christ Jesus
unto good works, which God hath before ordained
that we should walk in them." [2]   And again, after
a short interval : " At that time ye were without
Christ, being aliens from the commonwealth of
Israel, and strangers from the covenants of promise, having no hope, and without God in the
world : but now, in Christ Jesus, ye who were
sometimes far off are made nigh by the blood of
Christ.   For He is our peace, who hath made
both one, and hath broken down the middle wall
of partition between us ; having abolished in His
flesh the enmity, even the law of commandments
contained in ordinances ; for to make in Himself of twain one new man, so making peace ;
and that He might reconcile both unto God in
one body by the cross, having in Himself slain
the enmity ; and He came and preached peace
to you which were afar off, and to them that were
nigh.   For through Him we both have access by
one Spirit unto the Father." [3]   Then in another
passage he thus writes : " As the truth is in Jesus :
that ye put off, concerning the former conversation, the old man, which is corrupt according to
the deceitful lusts ; and be renewed in the spirit
of your mind ; and that ye put on the new man,
which after God is created in righteousness and
true holiness." [4]   And again : " Grieve not the
Holy Spirit of God, whereby ye are sealed unto
the day of redemption." [5]

CHAP. 47. — FROM THE EPISTLE TO THE
COLOSSIANS.

To the Colossians he addresses these words :
" Giving thanks unto the Father, which hath
made us meet to be partakers of the inheritance
of the saints in light : who hath delivered us
from the power of darkness, and hath translated
us into the kingdom of His dear Son ; in whom
we have redemption in the remission of our
sins." [6]   And again he says : " And ye are complete in Him, which is the head of all principality
and power : in whom also ye are circumcised
with the circumcision made without hands, in
putting off the body of the flesh by the circumcision of Christ ; buried with Him in baptism,
wherein also ye are risen with Him through the
faith of the operation of God, who hath raised
Him from the dead.   And you, when ye were
dead in your sins and the uncircumcision of your
flesh, hath He quickened together with Him,
having forgiven you all trespasses ; blotting out
the handwriting of the decree that was against
us, which was contrary to us, and took it out of
the way, nailing it to His cross ; and putting the
flesh off Him, [7] He made a show of principali-
ties and powers, confidently triumphing over
them in Himself." [8]

CHAP. 48. — FROM THE EPISTLES TO TIMOTHY.

And then to Timothy he says : " This is a
faithful saying, [9] and worthy of all acceptation,
that Christ Jesus came into the world to save
sinners ; of whom I am chief.   Howbeit for this
cause I obtained mercy, that in me first Jesus
Christ might show forth all long-suffering, for a
pattern to them which should hereafter believe
on Him to life everlasting." [10]   He also says : " For
there is one God and one Mediator between God
and men, the man Christ Jesus ; who gave Himself a ransom for all." [11]   In his second Epistle
to the same Timothy, he says : " Be not thou
therefore ashamed of the testimony of our Lord,
nor of me His prisoner : but be thou a fellow-
labourer for the gospel, according to the power
of God ; who hath saved us, and called us with
a holy calling, not according to our works, but
according to His own purpose and grace, which
was given us in Christ Jesus before the world
began ; but is now manifested by the coming of
our Lord Jesus Christ, who hath abolished death,
and hath brought life and immortality to light
through the gospel." [12]

CHAP. 49. — FROM THE EPISTLE TO TITUS.

Then again he writes to Titus as follows :
" Looking for that blessed hope, and the glori-
ous appearing of the great God and our Saviour
Jesus Christ ; who gave himself for us, that He
might redeem us from all iniquity, and purify
unto Himself a peculiar people, zealous of good

---

1 Eph. ii. 1–5.
2 Eph. ii. 8–10.
3 Eph. ii. 12–18.
4 Eph. iv. 21–24.
5 Eph. iv. 30.
6 Col. i. 12–14.
7 Exuens se carnem.
8 Col. ii. 10–15.
9 Humanus sermo.
10 1 Tim. i. 15, 16.
11 1 Tim. ii. 5, 6.
12 2 Tim. i. 8–10.

works." [1]   And to the like effect in another passage : " But after that the kindness and love of God our Saviour toward man appeared, not by works of righteousness which we have done, but according to His mercy He saved us, by the washing of regeneration, and renewing of the Holy Ghost ; which He shed on us abundantly through Jesus Christ our Saviour ; that, being justified by His grace, we should be made heirs according to the hope of eternal life." [3]

CHAP. 50. — FROM THE EPISTLE TO THE HEBREWS.

Although the authority of the Epistle to the Hebrews is doubted by some,[3] nevertheless, as I find it sometimes thought by persons, who oppose our opinion touching the baptism of infants, to contain evidence in favour of their own views, we shall notice the pointed testimony it bears in our behalf ; and I quote it the more confidently, because of the authority of the Eastern Churches, which expressly place it amongst the canonical Scriptures.   In its very exordium one thus reads : " God, who at sundry times, and in divers manners, spake in time past unto the fathers by the prophets, hath in these last days spoken to us by His Son, whom He hath appointed heir of all things, by whom also He made the worlds ; who, being the brightness of His glory, and the express image of His person, and upholding all things by the word of His power, when He had by Himself purged our sins, sat down on the right hand of the Majesty on high." [4]   And by and by the writer says : " For if the word spoken by angels was stedfast, and every transgression and disobedience received a just recompense of reward, how shall we escape if we neglect so great salvation ? " [5]   And again in another passage : " Forasmuch then," says he, " as the children are partakers of flesh and blood, He also Himself likewise took part of the same ; that through death He might destroy him that had the power of death, that is, the devil ; and deliver them who through fear of death were all their lifetime subject to bondage." [6]   Again, shortly after, he says : " Wherefore in all things it behoved Him to be made like unto His brethren, that He might be a merciful and faithful High Priest in things pertaining

to God, to make reconciliation for the sins of the people." [7]   And in another place he writes : " Let us hold fast our profession.   For we have not a high priest which cannot be touched with the feeling of our infirmities ; but was in all points tempted like as we are, yet without sin." [8]   Again he says : " He hath an unchangeable priesthood. Wherefore He is able also to save them to the uttermost that come unto God by Him, seeing He ever liveth to make intercession for them.   For such a High Priest became us, who is holy, harmless, undefiled, separate from sinners, and made higher than the heavens ; who needeth not daily (as those high priests) to offer up sacrifice, first for His own sins, and then for the people's : for this He did once, when He offered up Himself." [9] And once more : " For Christ is not entered into the holy places made with hands, which are the figures of the true ; but into heaven itself, now to appear in the presence of God for us : nor yet that He should offer Himself often, as the high priest entereth into the holy place every year with blood of others ; (for then must He often have suffered since the foundation of the world ;) but now once, in the end of the world, hath He appeared to put away sin by the sacrifice of Himself.   And as it is appointed unto men once to die, but after this the judgment ; so Christ was once offered to bear the sins of many : and unto them that look for Him shall He appear the second time, without sin, unto salvation." [10]

CHAP. 51. — FROM THE APOCALYPSE.

The Revelation of John likewise tells us that in a new song these praises are offered to Christ : " Thou art worthy to take the book, and to open the seals thereof : for Thou wast slain, and hast redeemed us to God by Thy blood out of every kindred, and tongue, and people, and nation." [11]

CHAP. 52. — FROM THE ACTS OF THE APOSTLES.

To the like effect, in the Acts of the Apostles, the Apostle Peter designated the Lord Jesus as " the Author of life," upbraiding the Jews for having put Him to death in these words : " But ye dishonoured and denied the Holy One and the Just, and desired a murderer to be granted unto you, and ye killed the Author of life." [12] While in another passage he says : " This is the stone which was set at nought by you builders, which is become the head of the corner.   Neither is there salvation in any other : for there is none other name under heaven given among men whereby we must be saved." [13]   And again, else-

---

[1] Tit. ii. 13, 14.
[2] Tit. iii. 3-7.
[3] Amongst the Latins, as Jerome tells us in more than one passage (see his *Commentaries*, on Isa. vi., viii.; on Zech. viii.; on Matt. xxvi.; also, in his *Catal. Script. Eccles.*, c. xvi. [ad Paulum], and lxx. [ad Gaium], etc.).   The Greeks, however, held that the epistle was the work of St. Paul.   In his *Epistle* cxxix. [ad Dardanum] he thus writes: " We must admit that the epistle written to the Hebrews is regarded as the Apostle Paul's, not only by the churches of the East, but by all church writers who have from the beginning (*retro*) written in Greek." — NOTE OF THE BENEDICTINE EDITOR. [See Augustin's *City of God*, xvi. 22, and *Christian Doctrine*, ii. (8), 13.   The matter is fairly stated by Augustin, after whose day the Epistle was not doubted even in the West. — W.]
[4] Heb. i. 1-3.
[5] Heb. ii. 2, 3.
[6] Heb. ii. 14, 15.

[7] Heb. ii 17.
[8] Heb. iv. 14, 15.
[9] Heb. vii. 24-27.
[10] Heb. ix. 24-28.
[11] Rev v. 9.
[12] Acts iii. 14, 15.
[13] Acts iv. 11, 12.

where: "The God of our fathers raised up Jesus, whom ye slew, by hanging on a tree. Him hath God exalted with His right hand to be a Prince and a Saviour, for to give repentance to Israel, and forgiveness of sins."[1]   Once more: "To Him give all the prophets witness, that, through His name, whosoever believeth in Him shall receive remission of sins."[2]   Whilst in the same Acts of the Apostles Paul says: "Be it known therefore unto you, men and brethren, that through this Man is preached unto you the forgiveness of sins: and by Him every one that believeth is justified from all things, from which ye could not be justified by the law of Moses."[3]

CHAP. 53. — THE UTILITY OF THE BOOKS OF THE OLD TESTAMENT.

Under so great a weight of testimony, who would not be oppressed that should dare lift up his voice against the truth of God? And many other testimonies might be found, were it not for my anxiety to bring this tract to an end, — an anxiety which I must not slight. I have deemed it superfluous to quote from the books of the Old Testament, likewise, many attestations to our doctrine in inspired words, since what is concealed in them under the veil of earthly promises is clearly revealed in the preaching of the New Testament. Our Lord Himself briefly demonstrated and defined the use of the Old Testament writings, when He said that it was necessary that what had been written concerning Himself in the Law, and the Prophets, and the Psalms, should be fulfilled, and that this was that Christ must suffer, and rise from the dead the third day, and that repentance and remission of sins should be preached in His name among all nations, beginning at Jerusalem.[4] In agreement with this is that statement of Peter which I have already quoted, how that all the prophets bear witness to Christ, that at His hands every one that believes in Him receives remission of his sins.[2]

CHAP. 54. — BY THE SACRIFICES OF THE OLD TESTAMENT, MEN WERE CONVINCED OF SINS AND LED TO THE SAVIOUR.

And yet it is perhaps better to advance a few testimonies out of the Old Testament also, which ought to have a supplementary, or rather a cumulative value. The Lord Himself, speaking by the Psalmist, says: "As for my saints which are upon earth, He hath caused all my purposes to be admired in them."[5] Not *their merits*, but "*my purposes*." For what is theirs except that which is afterwards mentioned, —

"their weaknesses are multiplied,"[6] — above the weakness that they had? Moreover, the law also entered, that the offence might abound. But why does the Psalmist immediately add: "They hastened after?"[6] When their sorrows and infirmities multiplied (that is, when their offence abounded), they then sought the Physician more eagerly, in order that, where sin abounded, grace might much more abound. He then says: "I will not gather their assemblies together [with their offerings] of blood;" for by their many sacrifices of blood, when they gathered their assemblies into the tabernacle at first, and then into the temple, they were rather convicted as sinners than cleansed. I shall no longer, He says, gather their assemblies of blood-offerings together; because there is one blood-shedding given for many, whereby they may be truly cleansed. Then it follows: "Neither will I make mention of their names with my lips," as if they were the names of renewed ones. For these were their names at first: children of the flesh, children of the world, children of wrath, children of the devil, unclean, sinners, impious; but afterwards, children of God, — a new name to the new man, a new song to the singer of what is new, by means of the New Testament. Men must not be ungracious with God's grace, mean with great things; [but be ever rising] from the less to the greater. The cry of the whole Church is, "I have gone astray like a lost sheep."[7] From all the members of Christ the voice is heard: "All we, as sheep, have gone astray; and He hath Himself been delivered up for our sins."[8] The whole of this passage of prophecy is that famous one in Isaiah which was expounded by Philip to the eunuch of Queen Candace, and he believed in Jesus.[9] See how often he commends this very subject, and, as it were, inculcates it again and again on proud and contentious men: "He was a man under misfortune, and one who well knows to bear infirmities; wherefore also He turned away His face, He was dishonoured, and was not much esteemed. He it is that bears our weaknesses, and for us is involved in pains: and we accounted Him to be in pains, and in misfortune, and in punishment. But it was He who was wounded for our sins, was weakened for our iniquities; the chastisement of our peace was upon Him; and by His bruise we are healed. All we, as sheep, have gone astray; and the Lord delivered Him up for our sins. And although He was evilly entreated, yet He opened not His mouth: as a sheep was He led to the slaughter, and as a lamb is dumb before the shearer, so He opened not His mouth. In

---

[1] Acts v. 30, 31.
[2] Acts x. 43.
[3] Acts xiii. 38, 39.
[4] See Luke xxiv. 44-47.
[5] Ps. xvi. 3.

[6] Ps. xvi. 4.
[7] Ps. cxix. 176.
[8] Isa. liii. 6.
[9] Acts viii. 30-37.

His humiliation His judgment was taken away: His generation who shall declare? For His life shall be taken away from the earth, and for the iniquities of my people was He led to death. Therefore I will give the wicked for His burial, and the rich for His death; because He did no iniquity, nor deceit with His mouth. The Lord is pleased to purge Him from misfortune. If you could yourselves have given your soul on account of your sins, ye should see a seed of a long life. And the Lord is pleased to rescue His soul from pains, to show Him light, and to form it through His understanding; to justify the Just One, who serves many well; and He shall Himself bear their sins. Therefore He shall inherit many, and He shall divide the spoils of the mighty; and He was numbered amongst the transgressors; and Himself bare the sins of many, and He was delivered for their iniquities." [1] Consider also that passage of this same prophet which Christ actually declared to be fulfilled in Himself, when He recited it in the synagogue, in discharging the function of the reader: [2] "The Spirit of the Lord is upon me, because He hath anointed me: to preach glad tidings to the poor hath He sent me, that so I may refresh all who are broken-hearted, — to preach deliverance to the captives, and to the blind sight." [3] Let us then all acknowledge Him; nor should there be one exception among persons like ourselves, who wish to cleave to His body, to enter through Him into the sheepfold, and to attain to that life and eternal salvation which He has promised to His own. — Let us, I repeat, all of us acknowledge Him who did no sin, who bare our sins in His own body on the tree, that we might live with righteousness separate from sins; by whose scars we are healed, when we were weak [4] — like wandering sheep.

CHAP. 55 [XXVIII.] — HE CONCLUDES THAT ALL MEN NEED THE DEATH OF CHRIST, THAT THEY MAY BE SAVED. UNBAPTIZED INFANTS WILL BE INVOLVED IN THE CONDEMNATION OF THE DEVIL. HOW ALL MEN THROUGH ADAM ARE UNTO CONDEMNATION; AND THROUGH CHRIST UNTO JUSTIFICATION. NO ONE IS RECONCILED WITH GOD, EXCEPT THROUGH CHRIST.

In such circumstances, no man of those who have come to Christ by baptism has ever been regarded, according to sound faith and the true doctrine, as excepted from the grace of forgiveness of sins; nor has eternal life been ever thought possible to any man apart from His kingdom. For this [eternal life] is ready to be revealed at the last time, [5] that is, at the resurrection of the dead who are reserved not for that eternal death which is called "the second death," but for the eternal life which God, who cannot lie, promises to His saints and faithful servants. Now none who shall partake of this life shall be made alive except in Christ, even as all die in Adam. [6] For as none whatever, of all those who belong to the generation according to the will of the flesh, die except in Adam, in whom all sinned; so, out of these, none at all who are regenerated by the will of the Spirit are endowed with life except in Christ, in whom all are justified. Because as through one all to condemnation, so through One all to justification. [7] Nor is there any middle place for any man, and so a man can only be with the devil who is not with Christ. Accordingly, also the Lord Himself (wishing to remove from the hearts of wrong-believers [8] that vague and indefinite middle condition, which some would provide for unbaptized infants, — as if, by reason of their innocence, they were embraced in eternal life, but were not, because of their unbaptized state, with Christ in His kingdom) uttered that definitive sentence of His, which shuts their mouths: "He that is not with me is against me." [9] Take then the case of any infant you please: If he is already in Christ, why is he baptized? If, however, as the Truth has it, he is baptized just that he may be with Christ, it certainly follows that he who is not baptized is not with Christ; and because he is not "with" Christ, he is "against" Christ; for He has pronounced His own sentence, which is so explicit that we ought not, and indeed cannot, impair it or change it. And how can he be "against" Christ, if not owing to sin? for it cannot possibly be from his soul or his body, both of these being the creation of God. Now if it be owing to sin, what sin can be found at such an age, except the ancient and original sin? Of course that sinful flesh in which all are born to condemnation is one thing, and that Flesh which was made "after the likeness of sinful flesh," whereby also all are freed from condemnation, is another thing. It is, however, by no means meant to be implied that all who are born in sinful flesh are themselves actually cleansed by that Flesh which is "like" sinful flesh; "for all men have not faith;" [10] but that all who are born from the carnal union are born entirely of sinful flesh, whilst all who are born from the spiritual union are cleansed only by the Flesh which is in the likeness of sinful flesh.

---

[1] Isa. liii. 3–12.
[2] See Luke iv. 16–21.
[3] Isa. lxi. 1.
[4] There seems to be here some omission. — BENEDICTINE NOTE.
[5] 1 Pet. i. 5.
[6] 1 Cor. xv. 22.
[7] Rom. v. 18.
[8] Malè credentium.
[9] Matt. xii. 30.
[10] 2 Thess. iii. 2.

In other words, the former class are in Adam unto condemnation, the latter are in Christ unto justification. This is as if we should say, for example, that in such a city there is a certain midwife who delivers all; and in the same place there is an expert teacher who instructs all. By all, in the one case, only those who are born can possibly be understood; by all, in the other, only those who are taught: and it does not follow that all who are born also receive the instruction. But it is obvious to every one, that in the one case it is correctly said, " she delivers all," since without her aid no one is born; and in the other, it is rightly said, " he teaches all," since without his tutoring, no one learns.

CHAP. 56. — NO ONE IS RECONCILED TO GOD EXCEPT THROUGH CHRIST.

Taking into account all the inspired statements which I have quoted, — whether I regard the value of each passage one by one, or combine their united testimony in an accumulated witness or even include similar passages which I have not adduced, — there can be nothing discovered, but that which the catholic Church holds, in her dutiful vigilance against all profane novelties: that every man is separated from God, except those who are reconciled to God through Christ the Mediator; and that no one can be separated from God, except by sins, which alone cause separation; that there is, therefore, no reconciliation except by the remission of sins, through the one grace of the most merciful Saviour, — through the one sacrifice of the most veritable Priest; and that none who are born of the woman, that trusted the serpent and so was corrupted through desire,[1] are delivered from the body of this death, except by the Son of the virgin who believed the angel and so conceived without desire.[2]

CHAP. 57 [XXIX.] — THE GOOD OF MARRIAGE; FOUR DIFFERENT CASES OF THE GOOD AND THE EVIL USE OF MATRIMONY.

The good, then, of marriage lies not in the passion of desire, but in a certain legitimate and honourable measure in using that passion, appropriate to the propagation of children, not the gratification of lust.[3] That, therefore, which is disobediently excited in the members of the body of this death, and endeavours to draw into itself our whole fallen soul, (neither arising nor subsiding at the bidding of the mind), is that evil of sin in which every man is born. When, however, it is curbed from unlawful desires, and

is permitted only for the orderly propagation and renewal of the human race, this is the good of wedlock, by which man is born in the union that is appointed. Nobody, however, is born again in Christ's body, unless he be previously born in the body of sin. But inasmuch as it is evil to make a bad use of a good thing, so is it good to use well a bad thing. These two ideas therefore of *good* and *evil*, and those other two of a *good use* and an *evil use*, when they are duly combined together, produce four different conditions: — [1.] A man makes a good use of a good thing, when he dedicates his continence to God; [2.] He makes a bad use of a good thing, when he dedicates his continence to an idol; [3.] He makes a bad use of an evil thing, when he loosely gratifies his concupiscence by adultery; [4.] He makes a good use of an evil thing, when he restrains his concupiscence by matrimony. Now, as it is better to make good use of a good thing than to make good use of an evil thing, — since both are good, — so " he that giveth his virgin in marriage doeth well; but he that giveth her not in marriage doeth better."[4] This question, indeed, I have treated at greater length, and more sufficiently, as God enabled me according to my humble abilities, in two works of mine, — one of them, *On the Good of Marriage*, and the other, *On Holy Virginity*. They, therefore, who extol the flesh and blood of a sinful creature, to the prejudice of the Redeemer's flesh and blood, must not defend the evil of concupiscence through the good of marriage; nor should they, from whose infant age the Lord has inculcated in us a lesson of humility,[5] be lifted up into pride by the error of others. He only was born without sin whom a virgin conceived without the embrace of a husband, — not by the concupiscence of the flesh, but by the chaste submission of her mind.[6] She alone was able to give birth to One who should heal our wound, who brought forth the germ of a pure offspring without the wound of sin.

CHAP. 58 [XXX.] — IN WHAT RESPECT THE PELAGIANS REGARDED BAPTISM AS NECESSARY FOR INFANTS.

Let us now examine more carefully, so far as the Lord enables us, that very chapter of the Gospel where He says, " Except a man be born again, — of water and the Spirit, — he shall not enter into the kingdom of God."[7] If it were not for the authority which this sentence has with them, they would not be of opinion that infants ought to be baptized at all. This is their comment on the passage: " Because He does not say, ' Except a man be born again of water

---

[1] Gen. iii. 6.
[2] Luke i. 38.
[3] [The editions, but apparently no MSS., add here the somewhat sententious words: " Voluntas ista, non voluptas illa, nuptialis est," — which may, perhaps, be rendered: " Wedded desire is willingness, not wantonness." — W.]

[4] 1 Cor. vii. 38.
[5] Matt. xviii. 4.
[6] Luke i. 34, 38.
[7] John iii. 3, 5.

and the Spirit, he shall not have salvation or eternal life,' but He merely said, 'he shall not enter into the kingdom of God,' therefore infants are to be baptized, in order that they may be with Christ in the kingdom of God, where they will not be unless they are baptized. Should infants die, however, even without baptism, they will have salvation and eternal life, seeing that they are bound with no fetter of sin." Now in such a statement as this, the first thing that strikes one is, that they never explain *where the justice is* of separating from the kingdom of God that "image of God" which has no sin. Next, we ought to see whether the Lord Jesus, the one only good Teacher, has not in this very passage of the Gospel intimated, and indeed shown us, that it only comes to pass through the remission of their sins that baptized persons reach the kingdom of God; although to persons of a right understanding, the words, as they stand in the passage, ought to be sufficiently explicit: "Except a man be born again, he cannot see the kingdom of God;"[1] and: "Except a man be born of water and of the Spirit, he cannot enter into the kingdom of God."[2] For why should he be born again, unless to be renewed? From what is he to be renewed, if not from some old condition? From what old condition, but that in which "our old man is crucified with Him, that the body of sin might be destroyed?"[3] Or whence comes it to pass that "the image of God" enters not into the kingdom of God, unless it be that the impediment of sin prevents it? However, let us (as we said before) see, as earnestly and diligently as we are able, what is the entire context of this passage of the Gospel, on the point in question.

CHAP. 59.—THE CONTEXT OF THEIR CHIEF TEXT.

"Now there was," we read, "a man of the Pharisees, named Nicodemus, a ruler of the Jews: the same came to Jesus by night, and said unto Him, Rabbi, we know that thou art a teacher come from God: for no man can do these miracles that thou doest, except God be with him. Jesus answered and said unto him, Verily, verily, I say unto thee, Except a man be born again, he cannot see the kingdom of God. Nicodemus saith unto Him, How can a man be born when he is old? can he enter the second time into his mother's womb, and be born? Jesus answered, Verily, verily, I say unto thee, Except a man be born of water and of the Spirit, he cannot enter into the kingdom of God. That which is born of the flesh is flesh; and that which is born of the Spirit is spirit. Marvel not that I said unto thee, Ye must be born again.

The wind bloweth where it listeth, and thou hearest the sound thereof, but canst not tell whence it cometh, and whither it goeth: so is every one that is born of the Spirit. Nicodemus answered and said unto Him, How can these things be? Jesus answered and said unto him, Art thou a master of Israel, and knowest not these things? Verily, verily, I say unto thee, We speak that we do know, and testify that we have seen; and ye receive not our witness. If I have told you earthly things, and ye believe not, how shall ye believe if I tell you of heavenly things? And no man hath ascended up to heaven, but He that came down from heaven, even the Son of man which is in heaven. And as Moses lifted up the serpent in the wilderness,[4] even so must the Son of man be lifted up; that whosoever believeth in Him should not perish, but have eternal life. For God so loved the world, that He gave His only-begotten Son, that whosoever believeth in Him should not perish, but have everlasting life. For God sent not His Son into the world to condemn the world, but that the world through Him might be saved. He that believeth on Him is not condemned; but he that believeth not is condemned already, because he hath not believed in the name of the only-begotten Son of God. And this is the condemnation, that light is come into the world, and men loved darkness rather than light, because their deeds were evil. For every one that doeth evil hateth the light, neither cometh to the light, lest his deeds should be reproved. But he that doeth truth cometh to the light, that his deeds may be made manifest, that they are wrought in God."[5] Thus far the Lord's discourse wholly relates to the subject of our present inquiry; from this point the sacred historian digresses to another matter.

CHAP. 60 [XXXI.]—CHRIST, THE HEAD AND THE BODY; OWING TO THE UNION OF THE NATURES IN THE PERSON OF CHRIST, HE BOTH REMAINED IN HEAVEN, AND WALKED ABOUT ON EARTH; HOW THE ONE CHRIST COULD ASCEND TO HEAVEN; THE HEAD, AND THE BODY, THE ONE CHRIST.

Now when Nicodemus understood not what was being told him, he inquired of the Lord how such things could be. Let us look at what the Lord said to him in answer to his inquiry; for of course, as He deigns to answer the question, How can these things be? He will in fact tell us how spiritual regeneration can come to a man who springs from carnal generation. After noticing briefly the ignorance of one who assumed a superiority over others as a teacher, and having blamed the unbelief of all such, for not

---

[1] John iii. 3.
[2] John iii. 5.
[3] Rom. vi. 6.

[4] Num. xxi. 9.
[5] John iii. 1–21.

accepting His witness to the truth, He went on to inquire and wonder whether, as He had told them about earthly things and they had not believed they would believe heavenly things. He nevertheless pursues the subject, and gives an answer such as others should believe — though these refuse — to the question that he was asked, How these things can be? "No man," says He, "hath ascended up to heaven, but He that came down from heaven, even the Son of man which is in heaven."[1] Thus, He says, shall come the spiritual birth, — men, from being earthly, shall become heavenly; and this they can only obtain by being made members of me; so that he may ascend who descended, since no one ascends who did not descend. All, therefore, who have to be changed and raised must meet together in a union with Christ, so that the Christ who descended may ascend, reckoning His body (that is to say, His Church) as nothing else than Himself, because it is of Christ and the Church that this is most truly understood: "And they twain shall be one flesh;"[2] concerning which very subject He expressly said Himself, "So then they are no more twain, but one flesh."[3] To ascend, therefore, they would be wholly unable, since "no man hath ascended up to heaven, but He that came down from heaven, even the Son of man which is in heaven."[1] For although it was on earth that He was made the Son of man, yet He did not deem it unworthy of that divinity, in which, although remaining in heaven, He came down to earth, to designate it by the name of the Son of man, as He dignified His flesh with the name of Son of God: that they might not be regarded as if they were two Christs, — the one God, the other man,[4] — but one and the same God and man, — God, because "in the beginning was the Word, and the Word was with God, and the Word was God;"[5] and man, inasmuch as "the Word was made flesh and dwelt among us."[6] By this means — by the difference between His divinity and His humiliation — He remained in heaven as Son of God, and as Son of man walked on earth; whilst, by that unity of His person which made His two natures one Christ, He both walked as Son of God on earth, and at the same time as the very Son of man remained in heaven. Faith, therefore, in more credible things arises from the belief of such things as are more incredible. For if His divine nature, though a far more distant object, and more sublime in its incomparable diversity, had ability so to take upon itself the nature of man on our account as to become one Person, and whilst appearing as Son of man on earth in the weakness of the flesh, was able to remain all the while in heaven in the divinity which partook of the flesh, how much easier for our faith is it to suppose that other men, who are His faithful saints, become one Christ with the Man Christ, so that, when all ascend by His grace and fellowship, the one Christ Himself ascends to heaven who came down from heaven? It is in this sense that the apostle says, "As we have many members in one body, and all the members of the body, being many, are one body, so likewise is Christ."[7] He did not say, "So also is Christ's" — meaning Christ's body, or Christ's members — but his words are, "*So likewise is Christ*," thus calling the head and body one Christ.

CHAP. 61 [XXXII.] — THE SERPENT LIFTED UP IN THE WILDERNESS PREFIGURED CHRIST SUSPENDED ON THE CROSS; EVEN INFANTS THEMSELVES POISONED BY THE SERPENT'S BITE.

And since this great and wonderful dignity can only be attained by the remission of sins, He goes on to say, "And as Moses lifted up the serpent in the wilderness, even so must the Son of man be lifted up; that whosoever believeth in Him should not perish, but have eternal life."[8] We know what at that time happened in the wilderness. Many were dying of the bite of serpents: the people then confessed their sins, and, through Moses, besought the Lord to take away from them this poison; accordingly, Moses, at the Lord's command, lifted up a brazen serpent in the wilderness, and admonished the people that every one who had been serpent-bitten should look upon the uplifted figure. When they did so they were immediately healed.[9] What means the uplifted serpent but the death of Christ, by that mode of expressing a sign, whereby the thing which is effected is signified by that which effects it? Now death came by the serpent, which persuaded man to commit the sin, by which he deserved to die. The Lord, however, transferred to His own flesh not sin, as the poison of the serpent, but He did transfer to it death, that the penalty without the fault might transpire in the likeness of sinful flesh, whence, in the sinful flesh, both the fault might be removed and the penalty. As, therefore, it then came to pass that whoever looked at the raised serpent was both healed of the poison and freed from death, so also now, whosoever is conformed to the likeness of the death of Christ by faith in Him and His baptism, is freed both from sin by justification, and from death by resurrection. For this

---

[1] John iii. 13.
[2] Gen. ii. 24.
[3] Mark x. 8.
[4] This was the error which was subsequently condemned in the heresy of Nestorius.
[5] John i. 1.
[6] John i. 14.

[7] 1 Cor. xii. 12.
[8] John iii. 14, 15.
[9] Numb. xxi. 6–9.

is what He says : "That whosoever believeth in Him should not perish, but have eternal life." [1] What necessity then could there be for an infant's being conformed to the death of Christ by baptism, if he were not altogether poisoned by the bite of the serpent?

CHAP. 62 [XXXIII.] — NO ONE CAN BE RECONCILED TO GOD, EXCEPT BY CHRIST.

He then proceeds thus, saying : "God so loved the world, that He gave His only-begotten Son, that whosoever believeth in Him should not perish, but have everlasting life." [2] Every infant, therefore, was destined to perish, and to lose everlasting life, if through the sacrament of baptism he believed not in the only-begotten Son of God; while nevertheless, He comes not so that he may judge the world, but that the world through Him may be saved. This especially appears in the following clause, wherein He says, "He that believeth in Him is not condemned; but he that believeth not is condemned already, because he hath not believed in the name of the only-begotten Son of God." [3] In what class, then, do we place baptized infants but amongst believers, as the authority of the catholic Church everywhere asserts? They belong, therefore, among those who have believed; for this is obtained for them by virtue of the sacrament and the answer of their sponsors. And from this it follows that such as are not baptized are reckoned among those who have not believed. Now if they who are baptized are not condemned, these last, as not being baptized, are condemned. He adds, indeed : "But this is the condemnation, that light is come into the world, and men loved darkness rather than light." [4] Of what does He say, "Light is come into the world," if not of His own advent? and without the sacrament of His advent, how are infants said to be in the light? And why should we not include this fact also in "men's love of darkness," that as they do not themselves believe, so they refuse to think that their infants ought to be baptized, although they are afraid of their incurring the death of the body? "In God," however, he declares are the "works of him wrought, who cometh to the light," [5] because he is quite aware that his justification results from no merits of his own, but from the grace of God. "For it is God," says the apostle, "who worketh in you both to will and to do of His own good pleasure." [6] This then is the way in which spiritual regeneration is effected in all who come to Christ from their carnal generation. He explained it

Himself, and pointed it out, when He was asked, How these things could be? He left it open to no man to settle such a question by human reasoning, lest infants should be deprived of the grace of the remission of sins. There is no other passage leading to Christ; no man can be reconciled to God, or can come to God otherwise, than through Christ.

CHAP. 63 [XXXIV.] — THE FORM, OR RITE, OF BAPTISM. EXORCISM.

What shall I say of the actual form of this sacrament? I only wish some one of those who espouse the contrary side would bring me an infant to be baptized. What does my exorcism work in that babe, if he be not held in the devil's family? The man who brought the infant would certainly have had to act as sponsor for him, for he could not answer for himself. How would it be possible then for him to declare that he renounced the devil, if there was no devil in him? that he was converted to God, if he had never been averted from Him? that he believed, besides other articles, in the forgiveness of sins, if no sins were attributable to him? For my own part, indeed, if I thought that his opinions were opposed to this faith, I could not permit him to bring the infant to the sacraments. Nor can I imagine with what countenance before men, or what mind before God, he can conduct himself in this. But I do not wish to say anything too severe. That a false or fallacious form of baptism should be administered to infants, in which there might be the sound and semblance of something being done, but yet no remission of sins actually ensue, has been seen by some amongst them to be as abominable and hateful a thing as it was possible to mention or conceive. Then, again, in respect of the necessity of baptism to infants, they admit that even infants stand in need of redemption, — a concession which is made in a short treatise written by one of their party, — but yet there is not found in this work any open admission of the forgiveness of a single sin. According, however, to an intimation dropped in your letter to me, they now acknowledge, as you say, that a remission of sins takes place even in infants through baptism. No wonder; for it is impossible that *redemption* should be understood in any other way. Their own words are these : "It is, however, not originally, but in their own actual life, after they have been born, that they have begun to have sin."

CHAP. 64. — A TWOFOLD MISTAKE RESPECTING INFANTS.

You see how great a difference there is amongst those whom I have been opposing at such length and persistency in this work, — one of whom has

[1] John iii. 15.
[2] John iii. 16.
[3] John iii. 18.
[4] John iii. 19.
[5] John iii. 21.
[6] Phil. ii. 13.

written the book which contains the points I have refuted to the best of my ability. You see, as I was saying, the important difference existing between such of them as maintain that infants are absolutely pure and free from all sin, whether original or actual; and those who suppose that so soon as born infants have contracted actual sins of their own, from which they need cleansing by baptism. The latter class, indeed, by examining the Scriptures, and considering the authority of the whole Church as well as the form of the sacrament itself, have clearly seen that by baptism remission of sins accrues to infants; but they are either unwilling or unable to allow that the sin which infants have is original sin. The former class, however, have clearly seen (as they easily might) that in the very nature of man, which is open to the consideration of all men, the tender age of which we speak could not possibly commit any sin whatever in its own proper conduct; but, to avoid acknowledging original sin, they assert that there is no sin at all in infants. Now in the truths which they thus severally maintain, it so happens that they first of all mutually agree with each other, and subsequently differ from us in material aspect. For if the one party concede to the other that remission of sins takes place in all infants which are baptized, whilst the other concedes to their opponents that infants (as infant nature itself in its silence loudly proclaims) have as yet contracted no sin in their own living, then both sides must agree in conceding to us, that nothing remains but original sin, which can be remitted in baptism to infants.

CHAP. 65 [XXXV.] — IN INFANTS THERE IS NO SIN OF THEIR OWN COMMISSION.

Will this also be questioned, and must we spend time in discussing it, in order to prove and show how that by their own will — without which there can be no sin in their own life — infants could never commit an offence, whom all, for this very reason, are in the habit of calling *innocent?* Does not their great weakness of mind and body, their great ignorance of things, their utter inability to obey a precept, the absence in them of all perception and impression of law, either natural or written, the complete want of reason to impel them in either direction, — proclaim and demonstrate the point before us by a silent testimony far more expressive than any argument of ours? The very palpableness of the fact must surely go a great way to persuade us of its truth; for there is no place where I do not find traces of what I say, so ubiquitous is the fact of which we are speaking, — clearer, indeed, to perceive than any thing we can say to prove it.

CHAP. 66. — INFANTS' FAULTS SPRING FROM THEIR SHEER IGNORANCE.

I should, however, wish any one who was wise on the point to tell me what sin he has seen or thought of in a new-born infant, for redemption from which he allows baptism to be already necessary; what kind of evil it has in its own proper life committed by its own mind or body. If it should happen to cry and to be wearisome to its elders, I wonder whether my informant would ascribe this to iniquity, and not rather to unhappiness. What, too, would he say to the fact that it is hushed from its very weeping by no appeal to its own reason, and by no prohibition of any one else? This, however, comes from the ignorance in which it is so deeply steeped, by reason of which, too, when it grows stronger, as it very soon does, it strikes its mother in its little passion, and often her very breasts which it sucks when it is hungry. Well, now, these small freaks are not only borne in very young children, but are actually loved, — and this with what affection except that of the flesh,[1] by which we are delighted by a laugh or a joke, seasoned with fun and nonsense by clever persons, although, if it were understood literally, as it is spoken, they would not be laughed with as facetious, but at as simpletons? We see, also, how those simpletons whom the common people call *Moriones*[2] are used for the amusement of the sane; and that they fetch higher prices than the sane when appraised for the slave market. So great, then, is the influence of mere natural feeling, even over those who are by no means simpletons, in producing amusement at another's misfortune. Now, although a man may be amused by another man's silliness, he would still dislike to be a simpleton himself; and if the father, who gladly enough looks out for, and even provokes, such things from his own prattling boy, were to foreknow that he would, when grown up, turn out a fool, he would without doubt think him more to be grieved for than if he were dead. While, however, hope remains of growth, and the light of intellect is expected to increase with the increase of years, then the insults of young children even to their parents seem not merely not wrong, but even agreeable and pleasant. No prudent man, doubtless, could possibly approve of not only not forbidding in children such conduct in word or deed as this, as soon as they are able to be forbidden, but even of exciting them to it, for the vain amusement of their elders. For as soon as children are of an age to know their father and mother, they dare not use wrong words to either, unless permitted or bidden by either, or both.

[1] Carnali.
[2] See above, ch. 32.

But such things can only belong to such young children as are just striving to lisp out words, and whose minds are just able to give some sort of motion to their tongue. Let us, however, consider the depth of the ignorance rather of the new-born babes, out of which, as they advance in age, they come to this merely temporary stuttering folly,—on their road, as it were, to knowledge and speech.

CHAP. 67 [XXXVI.] — ON THE IGNORANCE OF INFANTS, AND WHENCE IT ARISES.

Yes, let us consider that darkness of their rational intellect, by reason of which they are even completely ignorant of God, whose sacraments they actually struggle against, while being baptized. Now my inquiry is, When and whence came they to be immersed in this darkness? Is it then the fact that they incurred it all *here*, and in this their own proper life forgat God through too much negligence, after a life of wisdom and religion in their mother's womb? Let those say so who dare; let them listen to it who wish to; let them believe it who can. I, however, am sure that none whose minds are not blinded by an obstinate adherence to a foregone conclusion can possibly entertain such an opinion. Is there then no evil in ignorance,—nothing which needs to be purged away? What means that prayer: "Remember not the sins of my youth and of my ignorance?"[1] For although those sins are more to be condemned which are knowingly committed, yet if there were no sins of ignorance, we should not have read in Scripture what I have quoted, "Remember not the sins of my youth and of my ignorance." Seeing now that the soul of an infant fresh from its mother's womb is still the soul of a human being,—nay, the soul of a rational creature,—not only untaught, but even incapable of instruction, I ask why, or when, or whence, it was plunged into that thick darkness of ignorance in which it lies? If it is man's nature thus to begin, and that nature is not already corrupt, then why was not Adam created thus? Why was he capable of receiving a commandment? and able to give names to his wife, and to all the animal creation? For of her he said, "She shall be called Woman;"[2] and in respect of the rest we read: "Whatsoever Adam called every living creature, that was the name thereof."[3] Whereas this one, although he is ignorant where he is, what he is, by whom created, of what parents born, is already guilty of offence, incapable as yet of receiving a commandment, and so completely involved and overwhelmed in a thick cloud of ignorance, that he cannot be aroused out of his sleep, so as to recognize even

these facts; but a time must be patiently awaited, until he can shake off this strange intoxication, as it were, (not indeed in a single night, as even the heaviest drunkenness usually can be, but) little by little, through many months, and even years; and until this be accomplished, we have to bear in little children so many things which we punish in older persons, that we cannot enumerate them. Now, as touching this enormous evil of ignorance and weakness, if in this present life infants have contracted it as soon as they were born, where, when, how, have they by the perpetration of some great iniquity become suddenly implicated in such darkness?

CHAP. 68 [XXXVII.] — IF ADAM WAS NOT CREATED OF SUCH A CHARACTER AS THAT IN WHICH WE ARE BORN, HOW IS IT THAT CHRIST, ALTHOUGH FREE FROM SIN, WAS BORN AN INFANT AND IN WEAKNESS?

Some one will ask, If this nature is not pure, but corrupt from its origin, since Adam was not created thus, how is it that Christ, who is far more excellent, and was certainly born without any sin of a virgin, nevertheless appeared in this weakness, and came into the world in infancy? To this question our answer is as follows: Adam was not created in such a state, because, as no sin from a parent preceded him, he was not created in sinful flesh. We, however, are in such a condition, because by reason of his preceding sin we are born in sinful flesh. While Christ was born in such a state, because, in order that He might for sin condemn sin, He assumed the likeness of sinful flesh.[4] The question which we are now discussing is not about Adam in respect of the size of his body, why he was not made an infant but in the perfect greatness of his members. It may indeed be said that the beasts were thus created likewise,—nor was it owing to their sin that their young were born small. Why all this came to pass we are not now asking. But the question before us has regard to the vigor of man's mind and his use of reason, by virtue of which Adam was capable of instruction, and could apprehend God's precept and the law of His commandment, and could easily keep it if he would; whereas man is now born in such a state as to be utterly incapable of doing so, owing to his dreadful ignorance and weakness, not indeed of body, but of mind,—although we must all admit that in every infant there exists a rational soul of the self-same substance (and no other) as that which belonged to the first man. Still this great infirmity of the flesh, clearly, in my opinion, points to a something, whatever it may be, that is penal. It raises the doubt whether, if the first human beings had not sinned,

---

[1] Ps. xxiv. 7.
[2] Gen. ii. 23.
[3] Gen. ii. 19.

[4] Rom. viii. 3.

they would have had children who could use neither tongue, nor hands, nor feet. That they should be born children was perhaps necessary, on account of the limited capacity of the womb. But, at the same time, it does not follow, because a rib is a small part of a man's body, that God made an infant wife for the man, and then built her up into a woman. In like manner, God's almighty power was competent to make her children also, as soon as born, grown up at once.

CHAP. 69 [XXXVIII.] — THE IGNORANCE AND THE INFIRMITY OF AN INFANT.

But not to dwell on this, that was at least possible to them which has actually happened to many animals, the young of which are born small, and do not advance in mind (since they have no rational soul) as their bodies grow larger, and yet, even when most diminutive, run about, and recognize their mothers, and require no external help or care when they want to suck, but with remarkable ease discover their mothers' breasts themselves, although these are concealed from ordinary sight. A human being, on the contrary, at his birth is furnished neither with feet fit for walking, nor with hands able even to scratch ; and unless their lips were actually applied to the breast by the mother, they would not know where to find it ; and even when close to the nipple, they would, notwithstanding their desire for food, be more able to cry than to suck. This utter helplessness of body thus fits in with their infirmity of mind ; nor would Christ's flesh have been "in the likeness of sinful flesh," unless that sinful flesh had been such that the rational soul is oppressed by it in the way we have described, — whether this too has been derived from parents, or created in each case for the individual separately, or inspired from above, — concerning which I forbear from inquiring now.

CHAP. 70 [XXXIX.] — HOW FAR SIN IS DONE AWAY IN INFANTS BY BAPTISM, ALSO IN ADULTS, AND WHAT ADVANTAGE RESULTS THEREFROM.

In infants it is certain that, by the grace of God, through *His* baptism who came in the likeness of sinful flesh, it is brought to pass that the sinful flesh is done away. This result, however, is so effected, that the concupiscence which is diffused over and innate in the living flesh itself is not removed all at once, so as to exist in it no longer ; but only that that might not be injurious to a man at his death, which was inherent at his birth. For should an infant live after baptism, and arrive at an age capable of obedience to a law, he finds there somewhat to fight against, and, by God's help, to overcome, if he has not received His grace in vain, and if he is not willing to be a reprobate. For not even to those who are of riper years is it given in baptism (except, perhaps, by an unspeakable miracle of the almighty Creator), that *the law of sin* which is in their members, warring against the law of their mind, should be entirely extinguished, and cease to exist ; but that *whatever of evil has been done, said, or thought* by a man whilst he was servant to a mind subject to its concupiscence, should be abolished, and regarded as if it had never occurred. The concupiscence itself, however, (notwithstanding the loosening of the bond of guilt in which the devil, by it, used to keep the soul, and the destruction of the barrier which separated man from his Maker,) remains in the contest in which we chasten our body and bring it into subjection, whether to be relaxed for lawful and necessary uses, or to be restrained by continence.[1] But inasmuch as the Spirit of God, who knows so much better than we do all the past, and present, and future of the human race, foresaw and foretold that the life of man would be such that "no man living should be justified in God's sight,"[2] it happens that through ignorance or infirmity we do not exert all the powers of our will against it, and so yield to it in the commission of sundry unlawful things, — becoming worse in proportion to the greatness and frequency of our surrender ; and better, in proportion to its unimportance and infrequency. The investigation, however, of the point in which we are now interested — whether there could possibly be (or whether in fact there is, has been, or ever will be) a man without sin in this present life, except Him who said, "The prince of this world cometh, and hath nothing in me "[3] — requires a much fuller discussion ; and the arrangement of the present treatise is such as to make us postpone the question to the commencement of another book.

[1] 1 Cor. ix. 27.
[2] Ps. cxliii. 2.
[3] John xiv. 30.

BOOK II.

IN WHICH AUGUSTIN ARGUES AGAINST SUCH AS SAY THAT IN THE PRESENT LIFE
THERE ARE, HAVE BEEN, AND WILL BE, MEN WHO HAVE ABSOLUTELY NO SIN AT
ALL. HE LAYS DOWN FOUR PROPOSITIONS ON THIS HEAD: AND TEACHES, FIRST,
THAT A MAN MIGHT POSSIBLY LIVE IN THE PRESENT LIFE WITHOUT SIN, BY THE
GRACE OF GOD AND HIS OWN FREE WILL; HE NEXT SHOWS THAT NEVERTHELESS
IN FACT THERE IS NO MAN WHO LIVES QUITE FREE FROM SIN IN THIS LIFE;
THIRDLY, HE SETS FORTH THE REASON OF THIS, — BECAUSE THERE IS NO MAN
WHO EXACTLY CONFINES HIS WISHES WITHIN THE LIMITS OF THE JUST REQUIRE-
MENT OF EACH CASE, WHICH JUST REQUIREMENT HE EITHER FAILS TO PERCEIVE,
OR IS UNWILLING TO CARRY OUT IN PRACTICE; IN THE FOURTH PLACE, HE PROVES
THAT THERE IS NOT, NOR HAS BEEN, NOR EVER WILL BE, A HUMAN BEING —
EXCEPT THE ONE MEDIATOR, CHRIST — WHO IS FREE FROM ALL SIN.

CHAP. 1 [I.] — WHAT HAS THUS FAR BEEN DWELT
ON; AND WHAT IS TO BE TREATED IN THIS
BOOK.

WE have, my dearest Marcellinus, discussed at
sufficient length, I think, in the former book the
baptism of infants, — how that it is given to
them not only for entrance into the kingdom of
God, but also for attaining salvation and eternal
life, which none can have without the kingdom
of God, or without that union with the Saviour
Christ, wherein He has redeemed us by His
blood. I undertake in the present book to discuss and explain the question, Whether there
lives in this world, or has yet lived, or ever will
live, any one without any sin whatever, except
"the one Mediator between God and man, the
Man Christ Jesus, who gave Himself a ransom
for all;"[1] — with as much care and ability as
He may Himself vouchsafe to me. And should
there occasionally arise in this discussion, either
inevitably or casually from the argument, any
question about the baptism or the sin of infants,
I must neither be surprised nor must I shrink
from giving the best answer I can, at such emer-
gencies, to whatever point challenges my attention.

CHAP. 2 [II.] — SOME PERSONS ATTRIBUTE TOO
MUCH TO THE FREEDOM OF MAN'S WILL; IGNO-
RANCE AND INFIRMITY.

A solution is extremely necessary of this question about a human life unassailed by any de-
ception or preoccupation of sin, in consequence
even of our daily prayers. For there are some
persons who presume so much upon the free
determination of the human will, as to suppose
that it need not sin, and that we require no
divine assistance, — attributing to our nature,
once for all, this determination of free will. An
inevitable consequence of this is, that we ought
not to pray "not to enter into temptation," —
that is, not to be overcome of temptation, either
when it deceives and surprises us in our *ignorance,* or when it presses and importunes us in
our *weakness.* Now how hurtful, and how pernicious and contrary to our salvation in Christ,
and how violently adverse to the religion itself
in which we are instructed, and to the piety
whereby we worship God, it cannot but be for
us not to beseech the Lord for the attainment
of such a benefit, but be rather led to think that
petition of the Lord's Prayer, "Lead us not
into temptation,"[2] a vain and useless insertion, —
it is beyond my ability to express in words.

CHAP. 3 [III.] — IN WHAT WAY GOD COMMANDS
NOTHING IMPOSSIBLE. WORKS OF MERCY, MEANS
OF WIPING OUT SINS.

Now these people imagine that they are acute
(as if none among us knew it) when they say,
that "if we have not the will, we commit no
sin; nor would God command man to do what
was impossible for human volition." But they
do not see, that in order to overcome certain
things, which are the objects either of an evil
desire or an ill-conceived fear, men need the

---

[1] 1 Tim. ii. 5, 6.

[2] Matt. vi. 13.

strenuous efforts, and sometimes even all the energies, of the will; and that we should only imperfectly employ these in every instance, He foresaw who willed so true an utterance to be spoken by the prophet: "In Thy sight shall no man living be justified." [1] The Lord, therefore, foreseeing that such would be our character, was pleased to provide and endow with efficacious virtue certain healthful remedies against the guilt and bonds even of sins committed after baptism,—for instance, the works of mercy,—as when he says: "Forgive, and ye shall be forgiven; give, and it shall be given unto you." [2] For who could quit this life with any hope of obtaining eternal salvation, with that sentence impending: "Whosoever shall keep the whole law, and yet offend in one point, he is guilty of all," [3] if there did not soon after follow: "So speak ye, and so do, as they that shall be judged by the law of liberty: for he shall have judgment without mercy that hath showed no mercy; and mercy rejoiceth against judgment?" [4]

CHAP. 4 [IV.] — CONCUPISCENCE, HOW FAR IN US; THE BAPTIZED ARE NOT INJURED BY CONCUPISCENCE, BUT ONLY BY CONSENT THEREWITH.

Concupiscence, therefore, as the law of sin which remains in the members of this body of death, is born with infants. In baptized infants, it is deprived of guilt, is left for the struggle [of life], [5] but pursues with no condemnation, such as die before the struggle. Unbaptized infants it implicates as guilty and as children of wrath, even if they die in infancy, draws into condemnation. In baptized adults, however, endowed with reason, whatever consent their mind gives to this concupiscence for the commission of sin is an act of their own will. After all sins have been blotted out, and that guilt has been cancelled which by nature [6] bound men in a conquered condition, it still remains,— but not to hurt in any way those who yield no consent to it for unlawful deeds,—until death is swallowed up in victory, [7] and, in that perfection of peace, nothing is left to be conquered. Such, however, as yield consent to it for the commission of unlawful deeds, it holds as guilty; and unless, through the medicine of repentance, and through works of mercy, by the intercession in our behalf of the heavenly High Priest, they be healed, it conducts us to the second death and utter condemnation. It was on this account that the Lord, when teaching us to pray, advised us, besides other petitions, to say: "Forgive us

our debts, as we forgive our debtors; and lead us not into temptation, but deliver us from evil." [8] For evil remains in our flesh, not by reason of the nature in which man was created by God and wisdom, but by reason of that offence into which he fell by his own will, and in which, since its powers are lost, he is not healed with the same facility of will as that with which he was wounded. Of this evil the apostle says: "I know that in my flesh dwelleth no good thing;" [9] and it is likewise to the same evil that he counsels us to give no obedience, when he says: "Let not sin therefore reign in your mortal body, to obey the lusts thereof." [10] When, therefore, we have by an unlawful inclination of our will yielded consent to these lusts of the flesh, we say, with a view to the cure of this fault, "Forgive us our debts;" [11] and we at the same time apply the remedy of a work of mercy, in that we add, "As we forgive our debtors." That we may not, however, yield such consent, let us pray for assistance, and say, "And lead us not into temptation;"—not that God ever Himself tempts any one with such temptation, "for God is not a tempter to evil, neither tempteth He any man;" [12] but in order that whenever we feel the rising of temptation from our concupiscence, we may not be deserted by His help, in order that thereby we may be able to conquer, and not be carried away by enticement. We then add our request for that which is to be perfected at the last, when mortality shall be swallowed up of life: [13] "But deliver us from evil." [14] For then there will exist no longer a concupiscence which we are bidden to struggle against, and not to consent to. The whole substance, accordingly, of these three petitions may be thus briefly expressed: "Pardon us for those things in which we have been drawn away by concupiscence; help us not to be drawn away by concupiscence; take away concupiscence from us."

CHAP. 5 [V.] — THE WILL OF MAN REQUIRES THE HELP OF GOD.

Now for the commission of sin we get no help from God; but we are not able to do justly, and to fulfil the law of righteousness in every part thereof, except we are helped by God. For as the bodily eye is not helped by the light to turn away therefrom shut or averted, but is helped by it to see, and cannot see at all unless it help it; so God, who is the light of the inner man, helps our mental sight, in order that we may do some good, not according to our own, but according to His righteousness. But if we turn

---

[1] Ps. cxliii. 2.
[2] Luke vi. 37, 38.
[3] Jas. ii. 10.
[4] Jas. ii. 12.
[5] See above, Book i. chap. 70 (xxxix.)
[6] Originaliter, i.e. owing to birth-sin.
[7] 1 Cor. xv. 54.

[8] Matt. vi. 12, 13.
[9] Rom. vii. 18.
[10] Rom. vi. 12.
[11] Matt. vi. 12.
[12] Jas. i. 13.
[13] 2 Cor. v. 4.
[14] Matt. vi. 13.

away from Him, it is our own act; we then are wise according to the flesh, we then consent to the concupiscence of the flesh for unlawful deeds. When we turn to Him, therefore, God helps us; when we turn away from Him, He forsakes us. But then He helps us even to turn to Him; and this, certainly, is something that light does not do for the eyes of the body. When, therefore, He commands us in the words, "Turn ye unto me, and I will turn unto you,"[1] and we say to Him, "Turn us, O God of our salvation,"[2] and again, "Turn us, O God of hosts;"[3] what else do we say than, "Give what Thou commandest?"[4] When He commands us, saying, "Understand now, ye simple among the people,"[5] and we say to Him, "Give me understanding, that I may learn Thy commandments;"[6] what else do we say than, "Give what Thou commandest?" When He commands us, saying, "Go not after thy lusts,"[7] and we say to Him, "We know that no man can be continent, except God gives it to him;"[8] what else do we say than, "Give what Thou commandest?" When He commands us, saying, "Do justice,"[9] and we say, "Teach me Thy judgments, O Lord;"[10] what else do we say than, "Give what Thou commandest?" In like manner, when He says: "Blessed are they which hunger and thirst after righteousness; for they shall be filled,"[11] from whom ought we to seek for the meat and drink of righteousness, but from Him who promises His fulness to such as hunger and thirst after it?

CHAP. 6. — WHEREIN THE PHARISEE SINNED WHEN HE THANKED GOD; TO GOD'S GRACE MUST BE ADDED THE EXERTION OF OUR OWN WILL.

Let us then drive away from our ears and minds those who say that we ought to accept the determination of our own free will and not pray God to help us not to sin. By such darkness as this even the Pharisee was not blinded; for although he erred in thinking that he needed no addition to his righteousness, and supposed himself to be saturated with abundance of it, he nevertheless gave thanks to God that he was not "like other men, unjust, extortioners, adulterers, or even as the publican; for he fasted twice in the week, he gave tithes of all that he possessed."[12] He wished, indeed, for no addition

to his own righteousness; but yet, by giving thanks to God, he confessed that all he had he had received from Him. Notwithstanding, he was not approved, both because he asked for no further food of righteousness, as if he were already filled, and because he arrogantly preferred himself to the publican, who was hungering and thirsting after righteousness. What, then, is to be said of those who, whilst acknowledging that they have no righteousness, or no fulness thereof, yet imagine that it is to be had from themselves alone, not to be besought from their Creator, in whom is its store and its fountain? And yet this is not a question about prayers alone, as if the energy of our will also should not be strenuously added. God is said to be "our Helper;"[13] but nobody can be helped who does not make some effort of his own accord. For God does not work our salvation in us as if He were working in insensate stones, or in creatures in whom nature has placed neither reason nor will. Why, however, He helps one man, but not another; or why one man so much, and another so much; or why one man in one way, and another in another, — He reserves to Himself according to the method of His own most secret justice, and to the excellency of His power.

CHAP. 7 [VI.] — FOUR QUESTIONS ON THE PERFECTION OF RIGHTEOUSNESS: (I.) WHETHER A MAN CAN BE WITHOUT SIN IN THIS LIFE.

Now those who aver that a man can exist in this life without sin, must not be immediately opposed with incautious rashness; for if we should deny the possibility, we should derogate both from the free will of man, who in his wish desires it, and from the power or mercy of God, who by His help effects it. But it is one question, whether he could exist; and another question, whether he does exist. Again, it is one question, if he does not exist when he could exist, why he does not exist; and another question, whether such a man as had never sinned at all, not only is in existence, but also could ever have existed, or can ever exist. Now, if in the order of this fourfold set of interrogative propositions, I were asked, [1st,] Whether it be possible for a man in this life to be without sin? I should allow the possibility, through the grace of God and the man's own free will; not doubting that the free will itself is ascribable to God's grace, in other words, to the gifts of God, — not only as to its existence, but also as to its being good, that is, to its conversion to doing the commandments of God. Thus it is that God's grace not only shows what ought to be done, but also helps to the possibility of doing what it shows. "What

[1] Zech. i. 3.
[2] Ps. lxxxv. 4.
[3] Ps. lxxx. 3, 4.
[4] Da quod jubes; see the Confessions, Book x. chap. 26.
[5] Ps. xciv. 8.
[6] Ps. cxix. 73.
[7] Ecclus. xviii. 30.
[8] Wisd. viii. 21.
[9] Isa. lvi. 1.
[10] Ps. cxix. 108.
[11] Matt. v. 6.
[12] Luke xviii. 11, 12.

[13] Ps. xl. 17, lxx. 5.

indeed have we that we have not received?"[1] Whence also Jeremiah says: "I know, O Lord, that the way of man is not in himself; it is not in man to walk and direct his steps."[2] Accordingly, when in the Psalms one says to God, "Thou hast commanded me to keep Thy precepts diligently,"[3] he at once adds not a word of confidence concerning himself but a wish to be able to keep these precepts: "O that my ways," says he, "were directed to keep Thy statutes! Then should I not be ashamed, when I have respect to all Thy commandments."[4] Now who ever wishes for what he has already so in his own power, that he requires no further help for attaining it? To whom, however, he directs his wish, — not to fortune, or fate, or some one else besides God, — he shows with sufficient clearness in the following words, where he says: "Order my steps in Thy word; and let not any iniquity have dominion over me."[5] From the thraldom of this execrable dominion they are liberated, to whom the Lord Jesus gave power to become the sons of God.[6] From so horrible a domination were they to be freed, to whom He says, "If the Son shall make you free, then shall ye be free indeed."[7] From these and many other like testimonies, I cannot doubt that God has laid no impossible command on man; and that, by God's aid and help, nothing is impossible, by which is wrought what He commands. In this way may a man, if he pleases, be without sin by the assistance of God.

CHAP. 8 [VII.] — (2) WHETHER THERE IS IN THIS WORLD A MAN WITHOUT SIN.

[2nd.] If, however, I am asked the second question which I have suggested, — whether there be a sinless man, — I believe there is not. For I rather believe the Scripture, which says: "Enter not into judgment with Thy servant; for in Thy sight shall no man living be justified."[8] There is therefore need of the mercy of God, which "exceedingly rejoiceth against judgment,"[9] and which that man shall not obtain who does not show mercy.[9] And whereas the prophet says, "I said, I will confess my transgressions unto the Lord, and Thou forgavest the iniquity of my heart,"[10] he yet immediately adds, "For this shall every saint pray unto Thee in an acceptable time."[11] Not indeed every sinner, but "every saint;" for it is the voice of saints which says, "If we say that we have no sin, we

deceive ourselves, and the truth is not in us."[12] Accordingly we read, in the Apocalypse of the same Apostle, of "the hundred and forty and four thousand" saints, "which were not defiled with women; for they continued virgins: and in their mouth was found no guile; for they are without fault."[13] "Without fault," indeed, they no doubt are for this reason, — because they truly found fault with themselves; and for this reason, "in their mouth was discovered no guile," — "because if they said they had no sin, they deceived themselves, and the truth was not in them."[12] Of course, where the truth was not, there would be guile; and when a righteous man begins a statement by accusing himself, he verily utters no falsehood.

CHAP. 9. — THE BEGINNING OF RENEWAL; RESURRECTION CALLED REGENERATION; THEY ARE THE SONS OF GOD WHO LEAD LIVES SUITABLE TO NEWNESS OF LIFE.

And hence in the passage, "Whosoever is born of God doth not sin, and he cannot sin, for His seed remaineth in him,"[14] and in every other passage of like import, they much deceive themselves by an inadequate consideration of the Scriptures. For they fail to observe that men severally become sons of God when they begin to live in newness of spirit, and to be renewed as to the inner man after the image of Him that created them.[15] For it is not from the moment of a man's baptism that all his old infirmity is destroyed, but renovation begins with the remission of all his sins, and so far as he who is now wise is spiritually wise. All things else, however, are accomplished in hope, looking forward to their being also realized in fact,[16] even to the renewal of the body itself in that better state of immortality and incorruption with which we shall be clothed at the resurrection of the dead. For this too the Lord calls a regeneration, — though, of course, not such as occurs through baptism, but still a regeneration wherein that which is now begun in the spirit shall be brought to perfection also in the body. "In the regeneration," says He, "when the Son of man shall sit in the throne of His glory, ye also shall sit upon twelve thrones, judging the twelve tribes of Israel."[17] For however entire and full be the remission of sins in baptism, nevertheless, if there was wrought by it at once, an entire and full change of the man into his everlasting newness, — I do not mean change in his body, which is now most clearly tending evermore to the old corruption and to death, after which it is to be renewed into

---

[1] 1 Cor. iv. 7.
[2] Jer. x. 23.
[3] Ps. cxix. 4.
[4] Ps. cxix. 5, 6.
[5] Ps. cxix. 133.
[6] John i. 12.
[7] John viii. 36.
[8] Ps. cxliii. 2.
[9] Jas. ii. 13.
[10] Ps. xxxii. 5.
[11] Ps. xxxii. 6.

[12] 1 John i. 8.
[13] Rev. xiv. 3–5.
[14] 1 John iii. 9.
[15] See Col. iii. 10.
[16] Donec etiam in re fiant.
[17] Matt. xix. 28.

a total and true newness, — but, the body being excepted, if in the soul itself, which is the inner man, a perfect renewal was wrought in baptism, the apostle would not say : "Even though our outward man perishes, yet the inward man is renewed day by day."[1] Now, undoubtedly, he who is still renewed day by day is not as yet wholly renewed; and in so far as he is not yet wholly renewed, he is still in his old state. Since, then, men, even after they are baptized, are still in some degree in their old condition, they are on that account also still children of the world; but inasmuch as they are also admitted into a new state, that is to say, by the full and perfect remission of their sins, and in so far as they are spiritually-minded, and behave correspondingly, they are the children of God. Internally we put off the old man and put on the new; for we then and there lay aside lying, and speak truth, and do those other things wherein the apostle makes to consist the putting off of the old man and the putting on of the new, which after God is created in righteousness and true holiness.[2] Now it is men who are already baptized and faithful whom he exhorts to do this, — an exhortation which would be unsuitable to them, if the absolute and perfect change had been already made in their baptism. And yet made it was, since we were then actually *saved;* for "He saved us by the laver of regeneration."[3] In another passage, however, he tells us how this took place. "Not they only," says he, "but ourselves also, which have the first-fruits of the Spirit, even we ourselves groan within ourselves, waiting for the adoption, to wit, the redemption of our body. For we are saved by hope: but hope that is seen is not hope; for what a man seeth, why doth he yet hope for? But if we hope for that we see not, then do we with patience wait for it."[4]

CHAP. 10 [VIII.] — PERFECTION, WHEN TO BE REALIZED.

Our full adoption, then, as children, is to happen at the redemption of our body. It is therefore the first-fruits of the Spirit which we now possess, whence we are already really become the children of God; for the rest, indeed, as it is by hope that we are saved and renewed, so are we the children of God. But inasmuch as we are not yet actually saved, we are also not yet fully renewed, nor yet also fully sons of God, but children of the world. We are therefore advancing in renewal and holiness of life, — and it is by this that we are children of God, and by this also we cannot commit sin; — until at last the whole of that by which we are kept as yet children of this world is changed into this; — for it is owing to this that we are as yet able to sin. Hence it comes to pass that "whosoever is born of God doth not commit sin;"[5] and as well, "if we were to say that we have no sin, we should deceive ourselves, and the truth would not be in us."[6] There shall be then an end put to that within us which keeps us children of the flesh and of the world; whilst that other shall be perfected which makes us the children of God, and renews us by His Spirit. Accordingly the same John says, "Beloved, now are we the sons of God; and it doth not yet appear what we shall be."[7] Now what means this variety in the expressions, "*we are,*" and "*we shall be,*" but this — *we are* in hope, *we shall be* in reality? For he goes on to say, "We know that when He shall appear, we shall be like Him, for we shall see Him as He is."[7] We have therefore even now begun to be like Him, having the first-fruits of the Spirit; but yet we are still unlike Him, by reason of the remainders of the old nature. In as far, then, as we are like Him, in so far are we, by the regenerating Spirit, sons of God; but in as far as we are unlike Him, in so far are we the children of the flesh and of the world. On the one side, we cannot commit sin; but, on the other, if we say that we have no sin, we only deceive ourselves, — until we pass entirely into the adoption, and the sinner be no more, and you look for his place and find it not.[8]

CHAP. 11 [IX.] — AN OBJECTION OF THE PELAGIANS : WHY DOES NOT A RIGHTEOUS MAN BEGET A RIGHTEOUS MAN?[9]

In vain, then, do some of them argue : "If a sinner begets a sinner, so that the guilt of original sin must be done away in his infant son by his receiving baptism, in like manner ought a righteous man to beget a righteous son." Just as if a man begat children in the flesh by reason of his righteousness, and not because he is moved thereto by the concupiscence which is in his members, and the law of sin is applied by the law of his mind to the purpose of procreation. His begetting children, therefore, shows that he still retains the old nature among the children of this world; it does not arise from the fact of his promotion to newness of life among the children of God. For "the children of this world beget and are begotten."[10] Hence also what is born of them is like them; for "that which is born of the flesh is flesh."[11] Only the children

[1] 2 Cor. iv. 16.
[2] Eph. iv. 24.
[3] Tit. iii. 5.
[4] Rom. viii. 23-25.

[5] 1 John iii. 9.
[6] 1 John i. 8.
[7] 1 John iii. 2.
[8] Ps. xxxvi. 10.
[9] [See below, c. 25; also *De Nuptiis,* i. 18; also *contra Julianum,* vi. 5.]
[10] Luke xx. 34.
[11] John iii. 6.

of God, however, are righteous ; but in so far as they are the children of God, they do not carnally beget, because it is of the Spirit, and not of the flesh, that they are themselves begotten. But as many of them as become parents, beget children from the circumstance that they have not yet put off the entire remains of their old nature in exchange for the perfect renovation which awaits them. It follows, therefore, that every son who is born in this old and infirm condition of his father's nature, must needs himself partake of the same old and infirm condition. In order, then, that he may be begotten again, he must also himself be renewed by the Spirit through the remission of sin ; and if this change does not take place in him, his righteous father will be of no use to him. For it is by the Spirit that he is righteous, but it is not by the Spirit that he begat his son. On the other hand, if this change does accrue to him, he will not be damaged by an unrighteous father : for it is by the grace of the Spirit that he has passed into the hope of the eternal newness ; whereas it is owing to his carnal mind that his father has wholly remained in the old nature.

CHAP. 12 [X.] — HE RECONCILES SOME PASSAGES OF SCRIPTURE.

The statement, therefore, "He that is born of God sinneth not," [1] is not contrary to the passage in which it is declared by those who are born of God, "If we say that we have no sin, we deceive ourselves, and the truth is not in us." [2] For however complete may be a man's present hope, and however real may be his renewal by spiritual regeneration in that part of his nature, he still, for all that, carries about a body which is corrupt, and which presses down his soul ; and so long as this is the case, one must distinguish even in the same individual the relation and source of each several action. Now, I suppose it is not easy to find in God's Scripture so weighty a testimony of holiness given of any man as that which is written of His three servants, Noah, Daniel, and Job, whom the Prophet Ezekiel describes as the only men able to be delivered from God's impending wrath. [3] In these three men he no doubt prefigures three classes of mankind to be delivered : in Noah, as I suppose, are represented righteous leaders of nations, by reason of his government of the ark as a type of the Church ; in Daniel, men who are righteous in continence ; in Job, those who are righteous in wedlock ; — to say nothing of any other view of the passage, which it is unnecessary now to consider. It is, at any rate, clear from this testimony of the prophet, and from other inspired

statements, how eminent were these worthies in righteousness. Yet no man must be led by their history to say, for instance, that drunkenness is not sin, although so good a man was overtaken by it ; for we read that Noah was once drunk, [4] but God forbid that it should be thought that he was an habitual drunkard.

CHAP. 13. — A SUBTERFUGE OF THE PELAGIANS.

Daniel, indeed, after the prayer which he poured out before God, actually says respecting himself, "Whilst I was praying and confessing my sins, and the sins of my people, before the Lord my God." [5] This is the reason, if I am not mistaken, why in the above-mentioned Prophet Ezekiel a certain most haughty person is asked, "Art thou then wiser than Daniel ? " [6] Nor on this point can that be possibly said which some contend for in opposition to the Lord's Prayer : "For although," they say, "that prayer was offered by the apostles, after they became holy and perfect, and had no sin whatever, yet it was not in behalf of their own selves, but of imperfect and still sinful men that they said, ' Forgive us our debts, as we also forgive our debtors.' They used the word *our*," they say, "in order to show that in one body are contained both those who still have sins, and themselves, who were already altogether free from sin." Now this certainly cannot be said in the case of Daniel, who (as I suppose) foresaw as a prophet this presumptuous opinion, when he said so often in his prayer, "We have sinned ;" and explained to us why he said this, not so as that we should hear from him, Whilst I was praying and confessing the sins of my people to the Lord, my God ; nor yet confounding distinction, so as that it would be uncertain whether he had said, on account of the fellowship of one body, While I was confessing *our* sins to the Lord my God ; but he expresses himself in language so distinct and precise, as if he were full of the distinction himself, and wanted above all things to commend it to our notice : "*My sins*," says he, "*and the sins of my people.*" Who can gainsay such evidence as this, but he who is more pleased to defend what he thinks than to find out what he ought to think ?

CHAP. 14. — JOB WAS NOT WITHOUT SIN.

But let us see what Job has to say of himself, after God's great testimony of his righteousness. "I know of a truth," he says, "that it is so : for how shall a mortal man be just before the Lord? For if He should enter into judgment with him, he would not be able to obey Him." [7] And shortly afterwards he asks : "Who shall resist His judgment? Even if I should seem righteous,

---

[1] 1 John iii. 9.
[2] 1 John i. 8.
[3] Ezek. xiv. 14

[4] Gen. ix. 21.
[5] Dan. ix. 20.
[6] Ezek. xxviii. 3.
[7] Job ix. 2, 3.

my mouth will speak profanely." [1] And again, further on, he says : "I know He will not leave me unpunished. But since I am ungodly, why have I not died? If I should wash myself with snow, and be purged with clean hands, thou hadst thoroughly stained me with filth." [2] In another of his discourses he says : "For Thou hast written evil things against me, and hast compassed me with the sins of my youth ; and Thou hast placed my foot in the stocks. Thou hast watched all my works, and hast inspected the soles of my feet, which wax old like a bottle, or like a moth-eaten garment. For man that is born of a woman hath but a short time to live, and is full of wrath ; like a flower that hath bloomed, so doth he fall ; he is gone like a shadow, and continueth not. Hast Thou not taken account even of him, and caused him to enter into judgment with Thee? For who is pure from uncleanness? Not even one ; even should his life last but a day." [3] Then a little afterwards he says : "Thou hast numbered all my necessities ; and not one of my sins hath escaped Thee. Thou hast sealed up my transgressions in a bag, and hast marked whatever I have done unwillingly." [4] See how Job, too, confesses his sins, and says how sure he is that there is none righteous before the Lord. So he is sure of this also, that if we say we have no sin, the truth is not in us. While, therefore, God bestows on him His high testimony of righteousness, according to the standard of human conduct, Job himself, taking his measure from that rule of righteousness, which, as well as he can, he beholds in God, knows of a truth that so it is ; and he goes on at once to say, "How shall a mortal man be just before the Lord? For if He should enter into judgment with him, he would not be able to obey Him ;" in other words, if, when challenged to judgment, he wished to show that nothing could be found in him which He could condemn, "he would not be able to obey him," since he misses even that obedience which might enable him to obey Him who teaches that sins ought to be confessed. Accordingly [the Lord] rebukes certain men, saying, "Why will ye contend with me in judgment?" [5] This [the Psalmist] averts, saying, "Enter not into judgment with Thy servant ; for in Thy sight shall no man living be justified." [6] In accordance with this, Job also asks : "For who shall resist his judgment? Even if I should seem righteous, my mouth will speak profanely ;" which means : If, contrary to His judgment, I should call myself righteous, when His perfect rule of righteousness proves me to be unrighteous, then of a truth my mouth would speak profanely, because it would speak against the truth of God.

CHAP. 15. — CARNAL GENERATION CONDEMNED ON ACCOUNT OF ORIGINAL SIN.

He sets forth that this absolute weakness, or rather condemnation, of carnal generation is from the transgression of original sin, when, treating of his own sins, he shows, as it were, their causes, and says that "man that is born of a woman hath but a short time to live, and is full of wrath." Of what wrath, but of that in which all are, as the apostle says, "by nature," that is, by origin, "children of wrath," [7] inasmuch as they are children of the concupiscence of the flesh and of the world? He further shows that to this same wrath also pertains the death of man. For after saying, "He hath but a short time to live, and is full of wrath," he added, "Like a flower that hath bloomed, so doth he fall ; he is gone like a shadow, and continueth not." He then subjoins : "Hast Thou not caused him to enter into judgment with Thee? For who is pure from uncleanness? Not even one ; even should his life last but a day." In these words he in fact says, Thou hast thrown upon man, short-lived though he be, the care of entering into judgment with Thee. For how brief soever be his life, — even if it last but a single day, — he could not possibly be clean of filth ; and therefore with perfect justice must he come under Thy judgment. Then, when he says again, "Thou hast numbered all my necessities, and not one of my sins hath escaped Thee : Thou hast sealed up my transgressions in a bag, and hast marked whatever I have done unwillingly ;" is it not clear enough that even those sins are justly imputed which are not committed through allurement of pleasure, but for the sake of avoiding some trouble, or pain, or death? Now these sins, too, are said to be committed under some necessity, whereas they ought all to be overcome by the love and pleasure of righteousness. Again, what he said in the clause, "Thou hast marked whatever I have done unwillingly," may evidently be connected with the saying : "For what I would, that I do not ; but what I hate, that do I." [8]

CHAP. 16. — JOB FORESAW THAT CHRIST WOULD COME TO SUFFER ; THE WAY OF HUMILITY IN THOSE THAT ARE PERFECT.

Now it is remarkable [9] that the Lord Himself, after bestowing on Job the testimony which is expressed in Scripture, that is, by the Spirit of

---

1 Job ix. 19, 20.
2 Job ix. 30.
3 Job xiii. 26, to xiv. 5.
4 Job xiv 16, 17.
5 Jer. ii. 29.
6 Ps. cxliii 2.

7 Eph. ii. 3.
8 Rom. vii. 15.
9 Quid quod.

God, " In all the things which happened to him he sinned not with his lips before the Lord,"[1] did yet afterwards speak to him with a rebuke, as Job himself tells us : " Why do I yet plead, being admonished, and hearing the rebukes of the Lord?"[2] Now no man is justly rebuked unless there be in him something which deserves rebuke. [XI.] And what sort of rebuke is this, — which, moreover, is understood to proceed from the person of Christ our Lord? He recounts to him all the divine operations of His power, rebuking him under this idea, — that He seems to say to him, " Canst thou effect all these mighty works as I can?" But to what purpose is all this but that Job might understand (for this instruction was divinely inspired into him, that he might foreknow Christ's coming to suffer), — that he might understand how patiently he ought to endure all that he went through, since Christ, although, when He became man for us, He was absolutely without sin, and although as God He possessed so great power, did for all that by no means refuse to obey even to the suffering of death? When Job understood this with a purer intensity of heart, he added to his own answer these words : " I used before now to hear of Thee by the hearing of the ear ; but behold now mine eye seeth Thee : therefore I abhor myself and melt away, and account myself but dust and ashes."[3] Why was he thus so deeply displeased with himself? God's work, in that he was man, could not rightly have given him displeasure, since it is even said to God Himself, " Despise not Thou the work of Thine own hands."[4] It was indeed in view of that righteousness, in which he had discovered his own unrighteousness,[5] that he abhorred himself and melted away, and deemed himself dust and ashes, — beholding, as he did in his mind, the righteousness of Christ, in whom there could not possibly be any sin, not only in respect of His divinity, but also of His soul and His flesh. It was also in view of this righteousness which is of God that the Apostle Paul, although as " touching the righteousness which is of the law he was blameless," yet " counted all things " not only as loss, but even as dung.[6]

CHAP. 17 [XII.] — NO ONE RIGHTEOUS IN ALL THINGS.[7]

That illustrious testimony of God, therefore, in which Job is commended, is not contrary to the passage in which it is said, " In Thy sight shall no man living be justified ; "[8] for it does not lead us to suppose that in him there was nothing at all which might either by himself truly or by the Lord God rightly be blamed, although at the same time he might with no untruth be said to be a righteous man, and a sincere worshipper of God, and one who keeps himself from every evil work. For these are God's words concerning him : " Hast thou diligently considered my servant Job? For there is none like him on the earth, blameless, righteous, a true worshipper of God, who keeps himself from every evil work."[9] First, he is here praised for his excellence in comparison with all men on earth. He therefore excelled all who were at that time able to be righteous upon earth ; and yet, because of this superiority over others in righteousness, he was not therefore altogether without sin. He is next said to be " *blameless* " — no one could fairly bring an accusation against him in respect of his life ; " *righteous* " — he had advanced so greatly in moral probity, that no man could be mentioned on a par with him ; " *a true worshipper of God* " — because he was a sincere and humble confessor of his own sins ; " *who keeps himself from every evil work* " — it would have been wonderful if this had extended to every evil word and thought. How great a man indeed Job was, we are not told ; but we know that he was a just man ; we know, too, that in the endurance of terrible afflictions and trials he was great ; and we know that it was not on account of his sins, but for the purpose of demonstrating his righteousness, that he had to bear so much suffering. But the language in which the Lord commends Job might also be applied to him who " delights in the law of God after the inner man, whilst he sees another law in his members warring against the law of his mind ; "[10] especially as he says, " The good that I would I do not : but the evil which I would not, that I do. Now, if I do that I would not, it is no more I that do it, but sin that dwelleth in me."[11] Observe how he too after the inward man is separate from every evil work, because such work he does not himself effect, but the evil which dwells in his flesh ; and yet, since he does not have even that ability to delight in the law of God except from the grace of God, he, as still in want of deliverance, exclaims, " O wretched man that I am ! who shall deliver me from the body of this death? God's grace, through Jesus Christ our Lord ! "[12]

CHAP. 18 [XIII.] — PERFECT HUMAN RIGHTEOUSNESS IS IMPERFECT.

There are then on earth righteous men, there are great men, brave, prudent, chaste, patient,

---

[1] Job i. 22.
[2] Job xxxix. 34.
[3] Job xlii. 5, 6.
[4] Ps. cxxxviii. 8.
[5] Qua se noverat *injustum*. Several mss. have *justum* [*q. d.* " had discovered what his own righteousness was," — *i.e.* nothing].
[6] Phil iii. 6-8.
[7] See below, chap. 23.
[8] Ps. cxliii. 2.

[9] Job i. 8.
[10] Rom. vii. 22, 23.
[11] Rom. vii. 19, 20.
[12] Rom. vii. 24, 25.

pious, merciful, who endure all kinds of temporal evil with an even mind for righteousness' sake. If, however, there is truth — nay, because there is truth — in these words, " If we say we have no sin, we deceive ourselves," [1] and in these, " In Thy sight shall no man living be justified," they are not without sin ; nor is there one among them so proud and foolish as not to think that the Lord's Prayer is needful to him, by reason of his manifold sins.

CHAP. 19. — ZACHARIAS AND ELISABETH, SINNERS.

Now what must we say of Zacharias and Elisabeth, who are often alleged against us in discussions on this question, except that there is clear evidence in the Scripture [2] that Zacharias was a man of eminent righteousness among the chief priests, whose duty it was to offer up the sacrifices of the Old Testament? We also read, however, in the Epistle to the Hebrews, in a passage which I have already quoted in my previous book,[3] that Christ was the only High Priest who had no need, as those who were called high priests, to offer daily a sacrifice for his own sins first, and then for the people. " For such a High Priest," it says, " became us, righteous, harmless, undefiled, separate from sinners, and made higher than the heavens ; who needeth not daily, as those high priests, to offer up sacrifice, first for his own sins." [4] Amongst the priests here referred to was Zacharias, amongst them was Phinehas, yea, Aaron himself, from whom this priesthood had its beginning, and whatever others there were who lived laudably and righteously in this priesthood ; and yet all these were under the necessity, first of all, of offering sacrifice for their own sins, — Christ, of whose future coming they were a type, being the only one who, as an incontaminable priest, had no such necessity.

CHAP. 20. — PAUL WORTHY TO BE THE PRINCE OF THE APOSTLES, AND YET A SINNER.

What commendation, however, is bestowed on Zacharias and Elisabeth which is not comprehended in what the apostle has said about himself before he believed in Christ? He said that, " as touching the righteousness which is in the law, he had been blameless." [5] The same is said also of them : " They were both righteous before God, walking in all the commandments and ordinances of the Lord blameless." [6] It was because whatever righteousness they had in them was not a pretence before men that it is said accordingly, " They walked *before the Lord*."

But that which is written of Zacharias and his wife in the phrase, *in all the commandments and ordinances of the Lord*, the apostle briefly expressed by the words, *in the law*. For there was not one law for him and another for them previous to the gospel. It was one and the same law which, as we read, was given by Moses to their fathers, and according to which, also, Zacharias was priest, and offered sacrifices in his course. And yet the apostle, who was then endued with the like righteousness, goes on to say : " But what things were gain to me, those I counted loss for Christ. Yea doubtless, and I count all things but loss for the excellency of the knowledge of our Lord Jesus Christ ; for whose sake I have not only thought all things to be only detriments, but I have even counted them as dung, that I may win Christ, and be found in Him, not having my own righteousness, which is of the law, but that which is through the faith of Christ, the righteousness which is of God by faith : that I may know Him, and the power of His resurrection, and the fellowship of His suffering, being made comformable unto His death ; if by any means I might attain unto the resurrection of the dead." [7] So far, then, is it from being true that we should, from the words in which Scripture describes them, suppose that Zacharias and Elisabeth had a perfect righteousness without any sin, that we must even regard the apostle himself, according to the selfsame rule, as not perfect, not only in that righteousness of the law which he possessed in common with them, and which he counts as loss and dung in comparison with that most excellent righteousness which is by the faith of Christ, but also in the very gospel itself, wherein he deserved the pre-eminence of his great apostleship. Now I would not venture to say this if I did not deem it very wrong to refuse credence to himself. He extends the passage which we have quoted, and says : " Not as though I had already attained, or were already perfect ; but I follow after, if I may comprehend that for which also I am apprehended in Christ Jesus. Brethren, I count not myself to have apprehended : but this one thing I do, forgetting those things which are behind, and reaching forth unto those things which are before, I press toward the mark, for the prize of the high calling of God in Christ Jesus." [8] Here he confesses that he has not yet attained, and is not yet perfect in that plenitude of righteousness which he had longed to obtain in Christ ; but that he was as yet pressing towards the mark, and, forgetting what was past, was reaching out to the things which are before him. We are sure, then, that what he says elsewhere is true even of himself : " Al-

---

[1] 1 John i. 8.
[2] Luke i. 6-9.
[3] See above, Book i. c. 50.
[4] Heb. vii. 26. 27.
[5] Phil. iii. 6.
[6] Luke i. 6. [See also his work, *De Gratia Christi*, 53.]
[7] Phil. iii. 7-11.
[8] Phil. iii. 12-14.

though our outward man is perishing, yet the inward man is renewed day by day." [1] Although he was already a perfect [2] traveller, he had not yet attained the perfect end of his journey. All such he would fain take with him as companions of his course. This he expresses in the words which follow our former quotation: "Let as many, then, of us as are perfect, be thus minded: and if ye be yet of another mind, God will reveal even this also to you. Nevertheless, whereunto we have already attained, let us walk by that rule." [3] This "walk" is not performed with the legs of the body, but with the affections of the soul and the character of the life, so that they who possess righteousness may arrive at perfection, who, advancing in their renewal day by day along the straight path of faith, have by this time become perfect as travellers in the self-same righteousness.

CHAP. 21 [XIV.] — ALL RIGHTEOUS MEN SINNERS.

In like manner, all who are described in the Scriptures as exhibiting in their present life good will and the actions of righteousness, and all who have lived like them since, although lacking the same testimony of Scripture; or all who are even now so living, or shall hereafter so live: all these are great, they are all righteous, and they are all really worthy of praise, — yet they are by no means without sin: inasmuch as, on the authority of the same Scriptures which make us believe in their virtues, we believe also that in "God's sight no man living is justified," [4] whence all ask that He will "not enter into judgment with His servants:" [4] and that not only to all the faithful in general, but to each of them in particular, the Lord's Prayer is necessary, which He delivered to His disciples. [5]

CHAP. 22 [XV.] — AN OBJECTION OF THE PELAGIANS; PERFECTION IS RELATIVE; HE IS RIGHTLY SAID TO BE PERFECT IN RIGHTEOUSNESS WHO HAS MADE MUCH PROGRESS THEREIN.

"Well, but," they say, "the Lord says, 'Be ye perfect even as your Father which is in heaven is perfect,' [6] — an injunction which He would not have given, if He had known that what He enjoined was impracticable." Now the present question is not whether it be possible for any men, during this present life, to be without sin if they receive that perfection for the purpose; for the question of possibility we have already discussed: [7] — but what we have now to consider is, whether any man in fact achieves perfection.

We have, however, already recognised the fact that no man wills as much as the duty demands, as also the testimony of the Scriptures, which we have quoted so largely above, declares. When, indeed, perfection is ascribed to any particular person, we must look carefully at the thing in which it is ascribed. For I have just above quoted a passage of the apostle, wherein he confesses that he was not yet perfect in the attainment of righteousness which he desired; but still he immediately adds, "Let as many of us as are perfect be thus minded." Now he would certainly not have uttered these two sentences if he had not been perfect in one thing, and not in another. For instance, a man may be perfect as a scholar in the pursuit of wisdom: and this could not yet be said of those to whom [the apostle] said, "I have fed you with milk, and not with meat: for hitherto ye have not been able to bear it, neither are ye yet able;" [8] whereas to those of whom it could be said he says, "Howbeit we speak wisdom among them that are perfect," — meaning, of course, "perfect pupils" to be understood. It may happen, therefore, as I have said, that a man may be already perfect as a scholar, though not as yet perfect as a teacher of wisdom; may be perfect as a learner, though not as yet perfect as a doer of righteousness; may be perfect as a lover of his enemies, though not as yet perfect in bearing their wrong. [9] Even in the case of him who is so far perfect as to love all men, inasmuch as he has attained even to the love of his enemies, it still remains a question whether he be perfect in that love, — in other words, whether he so loves those whom he loves as is prescribed to be exercised towards those to be loved, by the unchangeable love of truth. Whenever, then, we read in the Scriptures of any man's perfection, it must be carefully considered in what it is asserted, since a man is not therefore to be understood as being entirely without sin because he is described as perfect in some particular thing; although the term may also be employed to show, not, indeed, that there is no longer any point left for a man to reach his way to perfection, but that he has in fact advanced a very great way, and on that account may be deemed worthy of the designation. Thus, a man may be said to be perfect in the science of the law, even if there be still something unknown to him; and in the same manner the apostle called men perfect, to whom he said at the same time, "Yet if in anything ye be otherwise minded, God shall reveal even this to you. Nevertheless, whereto we have already attained, let us walk by the same rule." [10]

---

[1] 2 Cor. iv. 16.
[2] [Augustin plays on the word "perfect." — W.]
[3] Phil. iii. 15, 16.
[4] Ps. cxliii. 2.
[5] Matt. vi. 12; Luke xi. 4.
[6] Matt. v. 48.
[7] See above, chap. 7.

[8] 1 Cor. iii. 2.
[9] Ut sufferat is his antithesis here to ut diligat.
[10] Phil. iii. 15.

CHAP. 23 [XXI.] — WHY GOD PRESCRIBES WHAT HE KNOWS CANNOT BE OBSERVED.

We must not deny that God commands that we ought to be so perfect in doing righteousness, as to have no sin at all. Now that cannot be sin, whatever it may be, unless God has enjoined that it shall not be. Why then, they ask, does He command what He knows no man living will perform? In this manner it may also be asked, Why He commanded the first human beings, who were only two, what He knew they would not obey? For it must not be pretended that He issued that command, that some of us might obey it, if they did not; for, that they should not partake of the fruit of the particular tree, God commanded them, and none besides. Because, as He knew what amount of righteousness they would fail to perform, so did He also know what righteous measures He meant Himself to adopt concerning them. In the same way, then, He orders all men to commit no sin, although He knows beforehand that no man will fulfil the command; in order that He may, in the case of all who impiously and condemnably despise His precepts, Himself do what is just in their condemnation; and, in the case of all who while obediently and piously pressing on in his precepts, though failing to observe to the utmost all things which He has enjoined, do yet forgive others as they wish to be forgiven themselves, Himself do what is good in their cleansing. For how can forgiveness be bestowed by God's mercy on the forgiving, when there is no sin? or how prohibition fail to be given by the justice of God, when there is sin?

CHAP. 24. — AN OBJECTION OF THE PELAGIANS. THE APOSTLE PAUL WAS NOT FREE FROM SIN SO LONG AS HE LIVED.

"But see," say they, "how the apostle says, 'I have fought a good fight, I have kept the faith, I have finished my course: henceforth there is laid up for me a crown of righteousness;'[1] which he would not have said if he had any sin." It is for them, then, to explain how he could have said this, when there still remained for him to encounter the great conflict, the grievous and excessive weight of that suffering which he had just said awaited him.[2] In order to finish his course, was there yet wanting only a small thing, when in fact was still left to suffer wherein would be a fiercer and more cruel foe? If, however, he uttered such words of joy feeling sure and secure, because he had been made sure and secure by Him who had revealed to him the imminence of his suffering, then he spoke these words, not in the fulness of realiza-

tion, but in the firmness of hope, and represents what he foresees is to come as if it had already been done. If, therefore, he had added to those words the further statement, "I have no longer any sin," we must have understood him as even then speaking of a perfection arising from a future prospect, not from an accomplished fact. For his having no sin, which they suppose was completed when he spoke these words, pertained to the finishing of his course; just in the same way as his triumphing over his adversary in the decisive conflict of his suffering had also reference to the finishing of his course, although this they must needs themselves allow remained yet to be effected, when he was speaking these words. The whole of this, therefore, we declare to have been as yet awaiting its accomplishment, at the time when the apostle, with his perfect trust in the promise of God, spoke of it all as having been already realized. For it was in reference to the finishing of his course that he forgave the sins of those who sinned against him, and prayed that his own sins might in like manner be forgiven him; and it was in his most certain confidence in this promise of the Lord, that he believed he should have no sin in that last end, which was still future, even when in his trustfulness he spoke of it as already accomplished. Now, omitting all other considerations, I wonder whether, when he uttered the words in which he is thought to imply that he had no sin, that "thorn of the flesh" had been already removed from him, for the taking away of which he had three times entreated the Lord, and had received this answer: "My grace is sufficient for thee; for my strength is made perfect in weakness."[3] For bringing so great a man to perfection, it was needful that that "messenger of Satan" should not be taken away by whom he was therefore to be buffeted, "lest he should be unduly exalted by the abundance of his revelations,"[4] and is there then any man so bold as either to think or to say, that any one who has to bend beneath the burden of this life is altogether clean from all sin whatever?

CHAP. 25. — GOD PUNISHES BOTH IN WRATH AND IN MERCY.

Although there are some men who are so eminent in righteousness that God speaks to them out of His cloudy pillar, such as "Moses and Aaron among His priests, and Samuel among them that call upon His name,"[5] the latter of whom is much praised for his piety and purity in the Scriptures of truth, from his earliest childhood, in which his mother, to accomplish her vow, placed him in God's temple, and devoted

---

[1] 2 Tim. iv. 7.
[2] 2 Tim. iv. 6.

[3] 2 Cor. xii. 8, 9.
[4] 2 Cor. xii. 7.
[5] Ps. xcix. 6.

him to the Lord as His servant; — yet even of such men it is written, " Thou, O God, wast propitious unto them, though Thou didst punish all their devices." [1] Now the children of wrath God punishes in anger; whereas it is in mercy that He punishes the children of grace; since " whom He loveth He correcteth, and scourgeth every son whom He receiveth." [2] However, there are no punishments, no correction, no scourge of God, but what are owing to sin, except in the case of Him who prepared His back for the smiter, in order that He might experience all things in our likeness without sin, in order that He might be the saintly Priest of saints, making intercession even for saints, who with no sacrifice of truth say each one even for himself, " Forgive us our trespasses, even as we also forgive them that trespass against us." [3] Wherefore even our opponents in this controversy, whilst they are chaste in their life, and commendable in character, and although they do not hesitate to do that which the Lord enjoined on the rich man, who inquired of Him about the attainment of eternal life, after he had told Him, in answer to His first question, that he had already fully kept every commandment in the law, — that " if he wished to be perfect, he must sell all that he had and give to the poor, and transfer his treasure to heaven; " [4] yet they do not in any one instance venture to say that they are without sin. But this, as we believe, they refrain from saying, with deceitful intent; but if they are lying, in this very act they begin either to augment or commit sin.

CHAP. 26 [XVII.] — (3) [5] WHY NO ONE IN THIS LIFE IS WITHOUT SIN.

[3d.] [5] Let us now consider the point which I mentioned as our third inquiry. Since by divine grace assisting the human will, man may possibly exist in this life without sin, why does he not? To this question I might very easily and truthfully answer : Because men are unwilling. But if I am asked why they are unwilling, we are drawn into a lengthy statement. And yet, without prejudice to a more careful examination, I may briefly say this much : Men are unwilling to do what is right, either because what is right is unknown to them, or because it is unpleasant to them. For we desire a thing more ardently in proportion to the certainty of our knowledge of its goodness, and the warmth of our delight in it. Ignorance, therefore, and infirmity are faults which impede the will from moving either for doing a good work, or for refraining from an evil one. But that what was hidden may come to

light, and what was unpleasant may be made agreeable, is of the grace of God which helps the wills of men ; and that they are not helped by it, has its cause likewise in themselves, not in God, whether they be predestinated to condemnation, on account of the iniquity of their pride, or whether they are to be judged and disciplined contrary to their very pride, if they are children of mercy. Accordingly Jeremiah, after saying, " I know, O Lord, that the way of man is not in himself, and that it belongeth not to any man to walk and direct his steps," [6] immediately adds, " Correct me, O Lord, but with judgment, and not in Thine anger ; " [7] as much as to say, I know that it is for my correction that I am too little assisted by Thee, for my footsteps to be perfectly directed : but yet do not in this so deal with me as Thou dost in Thine anger, when Thou dost determine to condemn the wicked ; but as Thou dost in Thy judgment whereby Thou dost teach Thy children not to be proud. Whence in another passage it is said, " And Thy judgments shall help me." [8]

CHAP. 27.[9] — THE DIVINE REMEDY FOR PRIDE.

You cannot therefore attribute to God the cause of any human fault. For of all human offences, the cause is pride. For the conviction and removal of this a great remedy comes from heaven. God in mercy humbles Himself, descends from above, and displays to man, lifted up by pride, pure and manifest grace in very manhood, which He took upon Himself out of vast love for those who partake of it. For, not even did even this One, so conjoined to the Word of God that by that conjunction he became at once the one Son of God and the same One the one Son of man, act by the antecedent merits of His own will. It behoved Him, without doubt, to be one ; had there been two, or three, or more, if this could have been done, it would not have come from the pure and simple gift of God, but from man's free will and choice.[10] This, then, is especially commended to us ; this, so far as I dare to think, is the divine lesson especially taught and learned in those treasures of wisdom and knowledge which are hidden in Christ. Every one of us, therefore, now knows, now does not know — now rejoices, now does not rejoice — to begin, continue, and complete our good work, in order that he may know that it is due not to his own will, but to the gift of God, that he either knows or rejoices ; and thus he is cured

---

[1] Ps. xcix. 8.
[2] Prov. iii. 12; Heb. xii. 6.
[3] Matt. vi. 12, 14; Luke xi. 4.
[4] Matt. xix. 12.
[5] See above, chs. 7 and 8.

[6] Jer. x. 23.
[7] Jer. x. 24.
[8] Ps. cxix. 175.
[9] See below, in ch. 33: also *De Naturâ et Gratiâ*, 29-32; and *De Corrept. et Gratia*, 10.
[10] [Augustin appears to say, in this obscure passage, that had there been two *persons*, instead of two *natures* only, in our blessed Lord's person, then no doubt salvation would have been due partly to a human cause. — W.]

of vanity which elated him, and knows how truly it is said not of this earth of ours, but spiritually, "The Lord will give kindness and sweet grace, and our land shall yield her fruit." [1]   A good work, moreover, affords greater delight, in proportion as God is more and more loved as the highest unchangeable Good, and as the Author of all good things of every kind whatever.   And that God may be loved, "His love is shed abroad in our hearts," not by ourselves, but "by the Holy Ghost that is given unto us." [2]

CHAP. 28 [XVIII.] — A GOOD WILL COMES FROM GOD.

Men, however, are laboring to find in our own will some good thing of our own, — not given to us by God; but how it is to be found I cannot imagine. The apostle says, when speaking of men's good works, "What hast thou that thou didst not receive? now, if thou didst receive it, why dost thou glory, as if thou hadst not received it?" [3]   But, besides this, even reason itself, which may be estimated in such things by such as we are, sharply restrains every one of us in our investigations so as that we may not so defend grace as to seem to take away free will, or, on the other hand, so assert free will as to be judged ungrateful to the grace of God, in our arrogant impiety.[4]

CHAP. 29. — A SUBTERFUGE OF THE PELAGIANS.

Now, with reference to the passage of the apostle which I have quoted, some would maintain it to mean that "whatever amount of good will a man has, must be attributed to God on this account, — namely, because even this amount could not be in him if he were not a human being. Now, inasmuch as he has from God alone the capacity of being any thing at all, and of being human, why should there not be also attributed to God whatever there is in him of a good will, which could not exist unless he existed in whom it is?"   But in this same manner it may also be said that a bad will also may be attributed to God as its author; because even it could not exist in man unless he were a man in whom it existed; but God is the author of his existence as man; and thus also of his bad will, which could have no existence if it had not a man in whom it might exist.   But to argue thus is blasphemy.

CHAP. 30. — ALL WILL IS EITHER GOOD, AND THEN IT LOVES RIGHTEOUSNESS, OR EVIL, WHEN IT DOES NOT LOVE RIGHTEOUSNESS.

Unless, therefore, we obtain not simply deter-mination of will, which is freely turned in this direction and that, and has its place amongst those natural goods which a bad man may use badly; but also a good will, which has its place among those goods of which it is impossible to make a bad use: — unless the impossibility is given to us from God, I know not how to defend what is said: "What hast thou that thou didst not receive?"   For if we have from God a certain free will, which may still be either good or bad; but the good will comes from ourselves; then that which comes from ourselves is better than that which comes from Him.   But inasmuch as it is the height of absurdity to say this, they ought to acknowledge that we attain from God even a good will.   It would indeed be a strange thing if the will could so stand in some mean as to be neither good nor bad; for we either love righteousness, and it is good, and if we love it more, more good, — if less, it is less good; or if we do not love it at all, it is not good.   And who can hesitate to affirm that, when the will loves not righteousness in any way at all, it is not only a bad, but even a wholly depraved will?   Since therefore the will is either good or bad, and since of course we have not the bad will from God, it remains that we have of God a good will; else, I am ignorant, since our justification is from it, in what other gift from Him we ought to rejoice.   Hence, I suppose, it is written, "The will is prepared of the Lord;" [5] and in the Psalms, "The steps of a man will be rightly ordered by the Lord, and His way will be the choice of his will;" [6] and that which the apostle says, "For it is God who worketh in you both to will and to do of His own good pleasure." [7]

CHAP. 31. — GRACE IS GIVEN TO SOME MEN IN MERCY; IS WITHHELD FROM OTHERS IN JUSTICE AND TRUTH.

Forasmuch then as our turning away from God is our own act, and this is evil will; but our turning to God is not possible, except He rouses and helps us, and this is good will, — what have we that we have not received?   But if we received, why do we glory as if we had not received?   Therefore, as "he that glorieth must glory in the Lord," [8] it comes from His mercy, not their merit, that God wills to impart this to some, but from His truth that He wills not to impart it to others.   For to sinners punishment is justly due, because "the Lord God loveth mercy and truth," [9] and "mercy and truth are met together;" [10] and "all the paths of the Lord are

1 Ps. lxxxv. 12.
2 Rom. v. 5.
3 1 Cor. iv. 7.
4 See *De Gratiâ Christi*, 52; and *De Gratiâ et Libero Arbi-*

5 Prov. viii. 35.
6 Ps. xxxvii. 23.
7 Phil. ii. 13.
8 Isa. xlv. 25; Jer. ix. 23, 24; 1 Cor. i. 31.
9 Ps. lxxxiv. 11.
10 Ps. lxxxv. 10.

mercy and truth." [1] And who can tell the numberless instances in which Holy Scripture combines these two attributes? Sometimes, by a change in the terms, *grace* is put for *mercy*, as in the passage, " We beheld His glory, the glory as of the Only-begotten of the Father, full of grace and truth." [2] Sometimes also *judgment* occurs instead of *truth*, as in the passage, " I will sing of mercy and judgment unto Thee, O Lord." [3]

CHAP. 32. — GOD'S SOVEREIGNTY IN HIS GRACE.

As to the reason why He wills to convert some, and to punish others for turning away, — although nobody can justly censure the merciful One in conferring His blessing, nor can any man justly find fault with the truthful One in awarding His punishment (as no one could justly blame Him, in the parable of the labourers, for assigning to some their stipulated hire, and to others unstipulated largess [4]), yet, after all, the purpose of His more hidden judgment is in His own power. [XIX.] So far as it has been given us, let us have wisdom, and let us understand that the good Lord God sometimes withholds even from His saints either the certain knowledge or the triumphant joy of a good work, just in order that they may discover that it is not from themselves, but from Him that they receive the light which illuminates their darkness, and the sweet grace which causes their land [5] to yield her fruit.

CHAP. 33. — THROUGH GRACE WE HAVE BOTH THE KNOWLEDGE OF GOOD, AND THE DELIGHT WHICH IT AFFORDS.

But when we pray Him to give us His help to do and accomplish righteousness, what else do we pray for than that He would open what was hidden, and impart sweetness to that which gave no pleasure? For even this very duty of praying to Him we have learned by His grace, whereas before it was hidden; and by His grace have come to love it, whereas before it gave us no pleasure, — so that "he who glorieth must glory not in himself, but in the Lord." To be lifted up, indeed, to pride, is the result of men's own will, not of the operation of God; for to such a thing God neither urges us nor helps us. There first occurs then in the will of man a certain desire of its own power, to become disobedient through pride. If it were not for this desire, indeed, there would be nothing difficult; and whenever man willed it, he might refuse without difficulty. There ensued, however, out of the penalty which was justly due such a defect, that henceforth it became difficult

to be obedient unto righteousness; and unless this defect were overcome by assisting grace, no one would turn to holiness; nor unless it were healed by efficient grace would any one enjoy the peace of righteousness. But whose grace is it that conquers and heals, but His to whom prayer is directed: " Convert us, O God of our salvation, and turn Thine anger away from us?" [6] And both if He does this, He does it in mercy, so that it is said of Him, " Not according to our sins hath He dealt with us, nor hath He recompensed us according to our iniquities;" [7] and when He refrains from doing this to any, it is in judgment that He refrains. And who shall say to Him, " What hast Thou done?" when with pious mind the saints sing to the praise of His mercy and judgment? Wherefore even in the case of His saints and faithful servants He applies to them a tardier cure in certain of their failings, in order that, while they are involved in these, a less pleasure than is sufficient for the fulfilling of righteousness in all its perfection may be experienced by them at any good they may achieve, whether hidden or manifest; so that in respect of His most perfect rule of equity and truth " no man living can be justified in His sight." [8] He does not in His own self, indeed, wish us to fall under condemnation, but that we should become humble; and He displays to us all the self-same grace of His own. Let us not, however, after we have attained facility in all things, suppose that to be our own which is really His; for that would be an error most antagonistic to religion and piety. Nor let us think that we should, because of His grace, continue in the same sins as of old; but against that very pride, on account of which we are humiliated in them, let us, above all things, both vigilantly strive and ardently pray Him, knowing at the same time that it is by His gift that we have the power thus to strive and thus to pray; so that in every case, while we look not at ourselves, but raise our hearts above, we may render thanks to the Lord our God, and whenever we glory, glory in Him alone.

CHAP. 34 [XX.] — (4) THAT NO MAN, WITH THE EXCEPTION OF CHRIST, HAS EVER LIVED, OR CAN LIVE WITHOUT SIN. [9]

[4th.] There now remains our fourth point, after the explanation of which, as God shall help us, this lengthened treatise of ours may at last be brought to an end. It is this: Whether the man who never has had sin or is to have it, not merely is now living as one of the sons of men, but even could ever have existed at any time, or will yet in time to come exist? Now it is altogether most

1 Ps. xxv. 10.
2 John i. 14.
3 Ps. ci. 1.
4 Matt. xx. 1-16.
5 i.e., the soil of their hearts; see above, at the end of ch. 27.

6 Ps. lxxxv. 4.
7 Ps. ciii. 10.
8 Ps. cxliii. 2.
9 See above, chs. 7, 8, 26.

certain that such a man neither does now live, nor has lived, nor ever will live, except the one only Mediator between God and men, the Man Christ Jesus. We have already said a good deal on this subject in our remarks on the baptism of infants; for if these have no sin, not only are there at present, but also there have been, and there will be, persons innumerable without sin. Now if the point which we treated of under the second head be truly substantiated, that there is in fact no man without sin,[1] then of course not even infants are without sin. From which the conclusion arises, that even supposing a man could possibly exist in the present life so far advanced in virtue as to have reached the perfect fulness of holy living which is absolutely free from sin, he still must have been undoubtedly a sinner previously, and must have been converted from the sinful state to this subsequent newness of life. Now when we were discussing the second head, a different question was before us from that which is before us under this fourth head. For then the point we had to consider was, Whether any man in this life could ever attain to such perfection as to be absolutely without sin by the grace of God, by the hearty desire of his own will? whereas the question now proposed in this fourth place is, Whether there be among the sons of men, or could possibly ever have been, or yet ever can be, a man who has not indeed emerged out of sin and attained to perfect righteousness, but has never, at any time whatever, been under the bondage of sin? If, therefore, the remarks are true which we have made at so great length concerning infants, there neither is, has been, nor will be, among the sons of men any such man, except the one Mediator, in whom there accrues to us propitiation and justification through which we have reconciliation with God, by the termination of the enmity produced by our sins. It will therefore be not unsuitable to retrace a few considerations, so far as the present subject seems to require, from the very commencement of the human race, in order that they may inform and strengthen the reader's mind in answer to some objections which may possibly disturb him.

CHAP. 35 [XXI.] — ADAM AND EVE; OBEDIENCE MOST STRONGLY ENJOINED BY GOD ON MAN.

When the first human beings — the one man Adam, and his wife Eve who came out of him — willed not to obey the commandment which they had received from God, a just and deserved punishment overtook them. The Lord had threatened that, on the day they ate the forbidden fruit, they should surely die.[2] Now, inasmuch as they had received the permission of using for food every tree that grew in Paradise, among which God had planted the tree of life, but had been forbidden to partake of one only tree, which He called the tree of knowledge of good and evil, to signify by this name the consequence of their discovering whether what good they would experience if they kept the prohibition, or what evil if they transgressed it: they are no doubt rightly considered to have abstained from the forbidden food previous to the malignant persuasion of the devil, and to have used all which had been allowed them, and therefore, among all the others, and before all the others, the tree of life. For what could be more absurd than to suppose that they partook of the fruit of other trees, but not of that which had been equally with others granted to them, and which, by its especial virtue, prevented even their animal bodies from undergoing change through the decay of age, and from aging into death, applying this benefit from its own body to the man's body, and in a mystery demonstrating what is conferred by wisdom (which it symbolized) on the rational soul, even that, quickened by its fruit, it should not be changed into the decay and death of iniquity? For of her it is rightly said, "She is a tree of life to them that lay hold of her."[3] Just as the one tree was for the bodily Paradise, the other is for the spiritual; the one affording a vigour to the senses of the outward man, the other to those of the inner man, such as will abide without any change for the worse through time. They therefore served God, since that dutiful obedience was committed to them, by which alone God can be worshipped. And it was not possible more suitably to intimate the inherent importance of obedience, or its sole sufficiency securely to keep the rational creature under the Creator, than by forbidding a tree which was not in itself evil. For God forbid that the Creator of good things, who made all things, "and behold they were very good,"[4] should plant anything evil amidst the fertility of even that material Paradise. Still, however, in order that he might show man, to whom submission to such a Master would be very useful, how much good belonged simply to obedience (and this was all that He had demanded of His servant, and this would be of advantage not so much for the lordship of the Master as for the profit of the servant), they were forbidden the use of a tree, which, if it had not been for the prohibition, they might have used without suffering any evil result whatever; and from this circumstance it may be clearly understood, that whatever evil they brought on themselves because they made use of it in spite of the prohibition, the tree did not produce from any noxious or pernicious quality

---

[1] See above, chs. 8, 9.
[2] Gen. ii. 17.
[3] Prov. iii. 18.
[4] Gen. i. 31.

in its fruit, but entirely on account of their violated obedience.

Chap. 36 [XXII.] — Man's state before the fall.

Before they had thus violated their obedience they were pleasing to God, and God was pleasing to them ; and though they carried about an animal body, they yet felt in it no disobedience moving against themselves. This was the righteous appointment, that inasmuch as their soul had received from the Lord the body for its servant, as it itself obeyed the Lord, even so its body should obey Him, and should exhibit a service suitable to the life given it without resistance. Hence "they were both naked, and were not ashamed."[1] It is with a natural instinct of shame that the rational soul is now indeed affected, because in that flesh, over whose service it received the right of power, it can no longer, owing to some indescribable infirmity, prevent the motion of the members thereof, notwithstanding its own unwillingness, nor excite them to motion even when it wishes. Now these members are on this account, in every man of chastity, rightly called "*pudenda*,"[2] because they excite themselves, just as they like, in opposition to the mind which is their master, as if they were their own masters ; and the sole authority which the bridle of virtue possesses over them is to check them from approaching impure and unlawful pollutions. Such disobedience of the flesh as this, which lies in the very excitement, even when it is not allowed to take effect, did not exist in the first man and woman whilst they were naked and not ashamed. For not yet had the rational soul, which rules the flesh, developed such a disobedience to its Lord, as by a reciprocity of punishment to bring on itself the rebellion of its own servant the flesh, along with that feeling of confusion and trouble to itself which it certainly failed to inflict upon God by its own disobedience to Him ; for God is put to no shame or trouble when we do not obey Him, nor are we able in any wise to lessen His very great power over us ; but we are shamed in that the flesh is not submissive to our government, — a result which is brought about by the infirmity which we have earned by sinning, and is called "the sin which dwelleth in our members."[3] But this sin is of such a character that it is the punishment of sin. As soon, indeed, as that transgression was effected, and the disobedient soul turned away from the law of its Lord, then its servant, the body, began to cherish a law of disobedience against it ; and then the man and the woman grew ashamed of their nakedness, when they perceived the rebellious

motion of the flesh, which they had not felt before, and which perception is called "the opening of their eyes ; "[4] for, of course, they did not walk about among the trees with closed eyes. The same thing is said of Hagar : "Her eyes were opened, and she saw a well."[5] Then the man and the woman covered their parts of shame, which God had made for them as members, but they had made parts of shame.

Chap. 37 [XXIII.] — The corruption of nature is by sin, its renovation is by Christ.

From this law of sin is born the flesh of sin, which requires cleansing through the sacrament of Him who came in the likeness of sinful flesh, that the body of sin might be destroyed, which is also called "the body of this death," from which only God's grace delivers wretched man through Jesus Christ our Lord.[6] For this law, the origin of death, passed on from the first pair to their posterity, as is seen in the labour with which all men toil in the earth, and the travail of women in the pains of childbirth. For these sufferings they merited by the sentence of God, when they were convicted of sin ; and we see them fulfilled not only in them, but also in their descendants, in some more, in others less, but nevertheless in all. Whereas, however, the primeval righteousness of the first human beings consisted in obeying God, and not having in their members the law of their own concupiscence against the law of their mind ; now, since their sin, in our sinful flesh which is born of them, it is obtained by those who obey God, as a great acquisition, that they do not obey the desires of this evil concupiscence, but crucify in themselves the flesh with its affections and lusts, in order that they may be Jesus Christ's, who on His cross symbolized this, and who gave them power through His grace to become the sons of God. For it is not to all men, but to as many as have received Him, that He has given to be born again to God of the Spirit, after they were born to the world by the flesh. Of these indeed it is written : "But as many as received Him, to them gave He power to become the sons of God ; which were born, not of the flesh, nor of blood, nor of the will of man, nor of the will of the flesh, but of God."[7]

Chap. 38 [XXIV.] — What benefit has been conferred on us by the incarnation of the Word ; Christ's birth in the flesh, wherein it is like and wherein unlike our own birth.

He goes on to add, "And the Word was made

---

[1] Gen. ii 25.
[2] i.e. "Parts of shame."
[3] Rom. vii. 17, 23.

[4] Gen. iii. 7.
[5] Gen. xxi. 19.
[6] Rom. vii. 24, 25.
[7] John i. 12, 13.

flesh, and dwelt among us ; " [1] as much as to say, A great thing indeed has been done among them, even that they are born again to God of God, who had before been born of the flesh to the world, although created by God Himself; but a far more wonderful thing has been done, that, although it accrued to them by nature to be born of the flesh, but by the divine goodness to be born of God, — in order that so great a benefit might be imparted to them, He who was in His own nature born of God, vouchsafed in mercy to be also born of the flesh ; — no less being meant by the passage, "And the Word was made flesh, and dwelt among us." Hereby, he says in effect, it has been wrought that we who were born of the flesh as flesh, by being afterwards born of the Spirit, may be spirit and dwell in God ; because also God, who was born of God, by being afterwards born of the flesh, became flesh, and dwelt among us. For the Word, which became flesh, was in the beginning, and was God with God.[2] But at the same time His participation in our inferior condition, in order to our participation in His higher state, held a kind of medium [3] in His birth of the flesh ; so that we indeed were born in sinful flesh, but He was born in the likeness of sinful flesh, — we not only of flesh and blood, but also of the will of man, and of the flesh, but He was born only of flesh and blood, not of the will of man, nor or the will of the flesh, but of God : we, therefore, to die on account of sin, He, to die on our account without sin. So also, just as His inferior circumstances, into which He descended to us, were not in every particular exactly the same with our inferior circumstances, in which He found us here ; so our superior state, into which we ascend to Him, will not be quite the same with His superior state, in which we are there to find Him. For we by His grace are to be made the sons of God, whereas He was evermore by nature the Son of God ; we, when we are converted, shall cleave to God, though not as His equals ; He never turned from God, and remains ever equal to God ; we are partakers of eternal life, He is eternal life. He, therefore, alone having become man, but still continuing to be God, never had any sin, nor did he assume a flesh of sin, though born of a maternal [4] flesh of sin. For what He then took of flesh, He either cleansed in order to take it, or cleansed by taking it. His virgin mother, therefore, whose conception was not according to the law of sinful flesh (in other words, not by the excitement of

carnal concupiscence), but who merited by her faith that the holy seed should be framed within her, He formed in order to choose her, and chose in order to be formed from her. How much more needful, then, is it for sinful flesh to be baptized in order to escape the judgment, when the flesh which was untainted by sin was baptized to set an example for imitation?

CHAP. 39 [XXV.] — AN OBJECTION OF THE PELAGIANS.

The answer, which we have already given,[5] to those who say, " If a sinner has begotten a sinner, a righteous man ought also to have begotten a righteous man," we now advance in reply to such as argue that one who is born of a baptized man ought himself to be regarded as already baptized. " For why," they ask, " could he not have been baptized in the loins of his father, when, according to the Epistle to the Hebrews, Levi,[6] was able to pay tithes in the loins of Abraham?" They who propose this argument ought to observe that Levi did not on this account subsequently not pay tithes, because he had paid tithes already in the loins of Abraham, but because he was ordained to the office of the priesthood in order to receive tithes, not to pay them ; otherwise neither would his brethren, who all contributed their tithes to him, have been tithed — because they too, whilst in the loins of Abraham, had already paid tithes to Melchisedec.

CHAP. 40. — AN ARGUMENT ANTICIPATED.

And let no one contend that the descendants of Abraham might fairly enough have paid tithes, although they had already paid tithes in the loins of their forefather, seeing that paying tithes was an obligation of such a nature as to require constant repetition from each several person, just as the Israelites used to pay such contributions every year all through life to their Levites, to whom were due various tithes from all kinds of produce ; whereas baptism is a sacrament of such a nature as is administered once for all, and if one had already received it when in his father, he must be considered as no other than baptized, since he was born of a man who had been himself baptized. Well, whoever thus argues (I will simply say, without discussing the point at length,) should look at circumcision, which was administered once for all, and yet was administered to each person separately and individually. Just as therefore it was necessary in the time of that ancient sacrament for the son of a circumcised man to be himself circumcised, so now the son of one who has been baptized must himself also receive baptism.

---

[1] John i. 14.
[2] John i. 1.
[3] Medietatem.
[4] De maternâ carne peccati, which is the reading of the best and oldest MSS. Another reading has, De naturâ carnis peccati (" of the nature of sinful flesh ") ; and a third, De materiâ carnis peccati (" of the matter of sinful flesh "). Compare Contr. Julianum, v. 9, and De Gen. ad. Lit. x. 18–20.

[5] See above, c. 11.
[6] The allusion is to Heb. vii. 9.

CHAP. 41. — CHILDREN OF BELIEVERS ARE CALLED "CLEAN" BY THE APOSTLE.[1]

The apostle indeed says, "Else were your children unclean, but now are they holy ; "[2] and "therefore" they infer "there was no necessity for the children of believers to be baptized." I am surprised at the use of such language by persons who deny that original sin has been transmitted from Adam. For, if they take this passage of the apostle to mean that the children of believers are born in a state of holiness, how is it that even they have no doubt about the necessity of their being baptized? Why, in fine, do they refuse to admit that any original sin is derived from a sinful parent, if some holiness is received from a holy parent? Now it certainly does not contravene our assertion, even if from the faithful "holy" children are propagated, when we hold that unless they are baptized those go into damnation, to whom our opponents themselves shut the kingdom of heaven, although they insist that they are without sin, whether actual or original.[3] Or, if they think it an unbecoming thing for "holy ones" to be damned, how can it be a becoming thing to exclude "holy ones" from the kingdom of God? They should rather pay especial attention to this point, How can something sinful help being derived from sinful parents, if something holy is derived from holy parents, and uncleanness from unclean parents? For the two-fold principle was affirmed when he said, "*Else were your children unclean, but now are they holy.*" They should also explain to us how it is right that the holy children of believers and the unclean children of unbelievers are, notwithstanding their different circumstances, equally prohibited from entering the kingdom of God, if they have not been baptized. What avails that sanctity of theirs to the one? Now if they were to maintain that the unclean children of unbelievers are damned, but that the holy children of believers are unable to enter the kingdom of heaven unless they are baptized, — but nevertheless are not damned, because they are "holy," — that would be some sort of a distinction ; but as it is, they equally declare respecting the holy children of holy parents and the unclean offspring of unclean parents, that they are not damned, since they have not any sin ; and that they are excluded from the kingdom of God because they are unbaptized. What an absurdity ! Who can suppose that such splendid geniuses do not perceive it?

CHAP. 42. — SANCTIFICATION MANIFOLD ; SACRAMENT OF CATECHUMENS.

Our opinions on this point are strictly in uni-son with the apostle's himself, who said, "From one all to condemnation," and "from one all to justification of life."[4] Now how consistent these statements are with what he elsewhere says, when treating of another point, "Else were your children unclean, but now are they holy," consider a while. [XXVI.] Sanctification is not of merely one measure ; for even catechumens, I take it, are sanctified in their own measure by the sign of Christ, and the prayer of imposition of hands ; and what they receive is holy, although it is not the body of Christ, — holier than any food which constitutes our ordinary nourishment, because it is a sacrament.[5] However, that very meat and drink, wherewithal the necessities of our present life are sustained, are, according to the same apostle, "sanctified by the word of God and prayer,"[6] even the prayer with which we beg that our bodies may be refreshed. Just as therefore this sanctification of our ordinary food does not hinder what enters the mouth from descending into the belly, and being ejected into the draught,[7] and partaking of the corruption into which everything earthly is resolved, whence the Lord exhorts us to labour for the other food which never perishes :[8] so the sanctification of the catechumen, if he is not baptized, does not avail for his entrance into the kingdom of heaven, nor for the remission of his sins. And, by parity of reasoning, that sanctification likewise, of whatever measure it be, which, according to the apostle, is in the children of believers, has nothing whatever to do with the question of baptism and of the origin or the remission of sin.[9] The apostle, in this very passage which has occupied our attention, says that the unbeliever of a married couple is sanctified by a believing partner : "For the unbelieving husband is sanctified by the wife, and the unbelieving wife is sanctified by the husband. Else were your children unclean, but now are they holy."[2] Now, I should say, there is not a man whose mind is so warped by unbelief, as to suppose that, whatever sense he gives to these words, they can possibly mean that a husband who is not a Christian should not be baptized, because his wife is a Christian, and that he has already obtained remission of his sins, with the certain prospect of entering the kingdom of heaven, because he is described as being sanctified by his wife.

---

[1] [See Gelasius, in his *Treatise against the Pelagians.*]
[2] 1 Cor. vii. 14.
[3] See above, Book i. chs 21-23.
[4] See Rom. v. 18.
[5] Catechumens received the *sacramentum salis* — salt placed in the mouth — with other rites, such as exorcism and the sign of the cross; the Lord's Prayer and other invocations concluding the ceremony. See Canon 5 of the third Council of Carthage; also Augustin's *De Catechiz. Rud.* 50; and his *Confessions*, i. 11, where (speaking of his own catechumenical course) he says: "I was now signed with the sign of His cross, and was *seasoned with His salt.*"
[6] 1 Tim. iv. 5.
[7] Mark vii. 19.
[8] John vi. 27.
[9] See below, Book iii. ch. 21; and his *Sermons*, xxix. 4.

CHAP. 43 [XXVII.] — WHY THE CHILDREN OF THE BAPTIZED SHOULD BE BAPTIZED.

If any man, however, is still perplexed by the question why the children of baptized persons are baptized, let him briefly consider this: Inasmuch as the generation of sinful flesh through the one man, Adam, draws into condemnation all who are born of such generation, so the generation of the Spirit of grace through the one man Jesus Christ, draws to the justification of eternal life all who, because predestinated, partake of this regeneration. But the sacrament of baptism is undoubtedly the sacrament of regeneration: Wherefore, as the man who has never lived cannot die, and he who has never died cannot rise again, so he who has never been born cannot be born again. From which the conclusion arises, that no one who has not been born could possibly have been born again in his father. Born again, however, a man must be, after he has been born; because, "Except a man be born again, he cannot see the kingdom of God"[1] Even an infant, therefore, must be imbued with the sacrament of regeneration, lest without it his would be an unhappy exit out of this life; and this baptism is not administered except for the remission of sins. And so much does Christ show us in this very passage; for when asked, How could such things be? He reminded His questioner of what Moses did when he lifted up the serpent. Inasmuch, then, as infants are by the sacrament of baptism conformed to the death of Christ, it must be admitted that they are also freed from the serpent's poisonous bite, unless we wilfully wander from the rule of the Christian faith. This bite, however, they did not receive in their own actual life, but in him on whom the wound was primarily inflicted.

CHAP. 44. — AN OBJECTION OF THE PELAGIANS.

Nor do they fail to see this point, that his own sins are no detriment to the parent after his conversion; they therefore raise the question: "How much more impossible is it that they should be a hinderance to his son?" But they who thus think do not attend to this consideration, that as his own sins are not injurious to the father for the very reason that he is born again of the Spirit, so in the case of his son, unless he be in the same manner born again, the sins which he derived from his father will prove injurious to him. Because even renewed parents beget children, not out of the first-fruits of their renewed condition, but carnally out of the remains of the old nature; and the children who are thus the offspring of their parents' remaining old nature, and are born in sinful flesh, escape from the condemnation which is due to the old man by the sacrament of spiritual regeneration and renewal. Now this is a consideration which, on account of the controversies that have arisen, and may still arise, on this subject, we ought to keep in our view and memory, — that a full and perfect remission of sins takes place only in baptism, that the character of the actual man does not at once undergo a total change, but that the first-fruits of the Spirit in such as walk worthily change the old carnal nature into one of like character by a process of renewal, which increases day by day, until the entire old nature is so renovated that the very weakness of the natural body attains to the strength and incorruptibility of the spiritual body.

CHAP. 45 [XXVIII.] — THE LAW OF SIN IS CALLED SIN; HOW CONCUPISCENCE STILL REMAINS AFTER ITS EVIL HAS BEEN REMOVED IN THE BAPTIZED.

This law of sin, however, which the apostle also designates "sin," when he says, "Let not *sin* therefore reign in your mortal body, that ye should obey it in the lusts thereof,"[2] does not so remain in the members of those who are born again of water and the Spirit, as if no remission thereof has been made, because there is a full and perfect remission of our sins, all the enmity being slain, which separated us from God; but it remains in our old carnal nature, as if overcome and destroyed, if it does not, by consenting to unlawful objects, somehow revive, and recover its own reign and dominion. There is, however, so clear a distinction to be seen between this old carnal nature, in which the law of sin, or sin, is already repealed, and that life of the Spirit, in the newness of which they who are baptized are through God's grace born again, that the apostle deemed it too little to say of such that they were not in sin; unless he also said that they were not in the flesh itself, even before they departed out of this mortal life. "They that are in the flesh," says he, "cannot please God; but ye *are not in the flesh*, but in the Spirit, if so be that the Spirit of God dwell in you."[3] And indeed, as they turn to good account the flesh itself, however corruptible it be, who apply its members to good works, and no longer are in that flesh, since they do not mould their understanding nor their life according to its principles; and as they in like manner make even a good use of death, which is the penalty of the first sin, who encounter it with fortitude and patience for their brethren's sake, and for the faith, and in defence of whatever is true and holy and just, — so also do all "true yokefellows" in the faith turn to good account that very law of sin which still remains, though remitted, in their old

[1] John iii. 3.

[2] Rom. vi. 12.
[3] Rom viii. 8, 9.

carnal nature, who, because they have the new life in Christ, do not permit lust to have dominion over them. And yet these very persons, because they still carry about Adam's old nature, mortally generate children to be immortally regenerated, with that propagation of sin, in which such as are born again are not held bound, and from which such as are born are released by being born again. As long, then, as the law by concupiscence[1] dwells in the members, although it remains, the guilt of it is released; but it is released only to him who has received the sacrament of regeneration, and has already begun to be renewed. But whatsoever is born of the old nature, which still abides with its concupiscence, requires to be born again in order to be healed. Seeing that believing parents, who have been both carnally born and spiritually born again, have themselves begotten children in a carnal manner, how could their children by any possibility, previous to their first birth, have been born again?

CHAP. 46.[2] — GUILT MAY BE TAKEN AWAY BUT CONCUPISCENCE REMAIN.

You must not be surprised at what I have said, that although the law of sin remains with its concupiscence, the guilt thereof is done away through the grace of the sacrament. For as wicked deeds, and words, and thoughts have already passed away, and cease to exist, so far as regards the mere movements of the mind and the body, and yet their guilt remains after they have passed away and no longer exist, unless it be done away by the remission of sins; so, contrariwise, in this law of concupiscence, which is not yet done away but still remains, its guilt is done away, and continues no longer, since in baptism there takes place a full forgiveness of sins. Indeed, if a man were to quit this present life immediately after his baptism, there would be nothing at all left to hold him liable, inasmuch as all which held him is released. As, on the one hand, therefore, there is nothing strange in the fact that the guilt of past sins of thought, and word, and deed remains before their remission; so, on the other hand, there ought to be nothing to create surprise, that the guilt of remaining concupiscence passes away after the remission of sin.

CHAP. 47 [XXIX.] — ALL THE PREDESTINATED ARE SAVED THROUGH THE ONE MEDIATOR CHRIST, AND BY ONE AND THE SAME FAITH.

This being the case, ever since the time when by one man sin thus entered into this world and death by sin, and so it passed through to all men, up to the end of this carnal generation and perishing world, the children of which beget and are begotten, there never has existed, nor ever will exist, a human being of whom, placed in this life of ours, it could be said that he had no sin at all, with the exception of the one Mediator, who reconciles us to our Maker through the forgiveness of sins. Now this same Lord of ours has never yet refused, at any period of the human race, nor to the last judgment will He ever refuse, this His healing to those whom, in His most sure foreknowledge and future loving-kindness, He has predestinated to reign with Himself to life eternal. For, previous to His birth in the flesh, and weakness in suffering, and power in His own resurrection, He instructed all who then lived, in the faith of those then *future* blessings, that they might inherit everlasting life; whilst those who were alive when all these things were being accomplished in Christ, and who were witnessing the fulfilment of prophecy, He instructed in the faith of these then *present* blessings; whilst again, those who have since lived, and ourselves who are now alive, and all those who are yet to live, He does not cease to instruct, in the faith of these now *past* blessings. It is therefore "one faith" which saves all, who after their carnal birth are born again of the Spirit, and it terminates in Him, who came to be judged for us and to die, — the Judge of quick and dead. But the sacraments of this "one faith" are varied from time to time in order to its suitable signification.

CHAP. 48. — CHRIST THE SAVIOUR EVEN OF INFANTS; CHRIST, WHEN AN INFANT, WAS FREE FROM IGNORANCE AND MENTAL WEAKNESS.

He is therefore the Saviour at once of infants and of adults, of whom the angel said, "There is born unto you this day a Saviour;"[3] and concerning whom it was declared to the Virgin Mary,[4] "Thou shalt call His name Jesus, for He shall save His people from their sins," where it is plainly shown that He was called Jesus because of the salvation which He bestows upon us, — Jesus being tantamount to the Latin *Salvator*, "Saviour." Who then can be so bold as to maintain that the Lord Christ is *Jesus* only for adults and not for infants also? who came in the likeness of sinful flesh, to destroy the body of sin, with infants' limbs fitted and suitable for no use in the extreme weakness of such body, and His rational soul oppressed with miserable ignorance! Now that such entire ignorance existed, I cannot suppose in the infant in whom the Word was made flesh, that He might dwell among us; nor can I imagine that such weakness of the mental faculty ever existed in the

---

[1] We follow the reading, *lex* [*scil.* peccati] *concupiscentialiter*, etc.

[2] Compare Augustin's *Contra Julianum*, vi. c. 22.

[3] Luke ii. 11.

[4] Rather to Joseph, Mary's husband; Matt. i. 21.

infant Christ which we see in infants generally. For it is owing to such infirmity and ignorance that infants are disturbed with irrational affections, and are restrained by no rational command or government, but by pains and penalties, or the terror of such; so that you can quite see that they are children of that disobedience, which excites itself in the members of our body in opposition to the law of the mind,—and refuses to be still, even when the reason wishes; nay, often is either repressed only by some actual infliction of bodily pain, as for instance by flogging; or is checked only by fear, or by some such mental emotion, but not by any admonishing of the will. Inasmuch, however, as in Him there was the likeness of sinful flesh, He willed to pass through the changes of the various stages of life, beginning even with infancy, so that it would seem as if even His flesh might have arrived at death by the gradual approach of old age, if He had not been killed while young. Nevertheless, the death is inflicted in sinful flesh as the due of disobedience, but in the likeness of sinful flesh it was undergone in voluntary obedience. For when He was on His way to it, and was soon to suffer it, He said, "Behold, the prince of this world cometh, and hath nothing in me. But that all may know that I am doing my Father's will, arise, let us go hence." [1] Having said these words, He went straightway, and encountered His undeserved death, having become obedient even unto death.

CHAP. 49 [XXX.]—AN OBJECTION OF THE PELAGIANS.

They therefore who say, "If through the sin of the first man it was brought about that we must die, by the coming of Christ it should be brought about that, believing in Him, we shall not die;" and they add what they deem a reason, saying, "For the sin of the first transgressor could not possibly have injured us more than the incarnation or redemption of the Saviour has benefited us." But why do they not rather give an attentive ear, and an unhesitating belief, to that which the apostle has stated so unambiguously: "Since by man came death, by Man came also the resurrection of the dead; for as in Adam all die, even so in Christ shall all be made alive?" [2] For it is of nothing else than of the resurrection of the body that he was speaking. Having said that the bodily death of all men has come about through one man, he adds the promise that the bodily resurrection of all men to eternal life shall happen through one, even Christ. How can it therefore be that "the one has injured us more by sinning than the other has benefited us by redeeming," when by the

sin of the former we die a temporal death, but by the redemption of the latter we rise again not to a temporal, but to a perpetual life? Our body, therefore, is dead because of sin, but Christ's body only died without sin, in order that, having poured out His blood without fault, "the bonds" [3] which contain the register of all faults "might be blotted out," by which they who now believe in Him were formerly held as debtors by the devil. And accordingly He says, "This is my blood, which is shed for many for the remission of sins." [4]

CHAP. 50 [XXXI.]—WHY IT IS THAT DEATH ITSELF IS NOT ABOLISHED, ALONG WITH SIN, BY BAPTISM.

He might, however, have also conferred this upon believers, that they should not even experience the death of their body. But if He had done this, there might no doubt have been added a certain felicity to the flesh, but the fortitude of faith would have been diminished; for men have such a fear of death, that they would declare Christians happy, for nothing else than their mere immunity from dying. And no one would, for the sake of that life which is to be so happy after death, hasten to the grace of Christ by the power of his contempt of death itself; but with a view to remove the trouble of death, would rather resort to a more delicate mode of believing in Christ. More grace, therefore, thàn this has He conferred on those who believe on Him; and a greater gift, undoubtedly, has He vouchsafed to them! What great matter would it have been for a man, on seeing that people did not die when they became believers, himself also to believe that he was not to die? How much greater a thing is it, how much braver, how much more laudable, so to believe, that although one is sure to die, he can still hope to live hereafter for evermore! At last, upon some there will be bestowed this blessing at the last day, that they shall not feel death itself in sudden change, but shall be caught up along with the risen in the clouds to meet Christ in the air, and so shall they ever live with the Lord. [5] And rightly shall it be these who receive this grace, since there will be no posterity after them to be led to believe, not by the hope of what they see not, but by the love of what they see. This faith is weak and nerveless, and must not be called faith at all, inasmuch as faith is thus defined: "Faith is the firmness of those who hope, [6] the clear proof of things which they do not see." [7] Accordingly, in the same Epistle to the Hebrews,

---

[1] John xiv. 30, 31.
[2] 1 Cor. xv. 21, 22.

[3] Col. ii. 14. Chirographa, i.e. "handwritings."
[4] Matt. xxvi. 28.
[5] 1 Thess. iv. 17. Compare *Retrac.* ii. 33 and Letter 193.
[6] Augustin constantly quotes this text with the active participle *sperantium*, instead of *sperandorum*. The Greek ἐλπιζομένων is not always construed passively in the passage: some regard it as of the middle voice.
[7] Heb. xi. 1.

where this passage occurs, after enumerating in subsequent sentences certain worthies who pleased God by their faith, he says : "These all died in faith, not having received the promises, but seeing them afar off, and hailing them, and confessing that they were strangers and pilgrims on the earth."[1] And then afterwards he concluded his eulogy on faith in these words : "And these all, having obtained a good report through faith, did not indeed receive God's promises ; for they foresaw better things for us, and that without us they could not themselves become perfect."[2] Now this would be no praise for faith, nor (as I said) would it be faith at all, were men in believing to follow after rewards which they could see,—in other words, if on believers were bestowed the reward of immortality in this present world.

CHAP. 51.—WHY THE DEVIL IS SAID TO HOLD THE POWER AND DOMINION OF DEATH.

Hence the Lord Himself willed to die, "in order that," as it is written of Him, "through death He might destroy him that had the power of death, that is, the devil ; and deliver them who through fear of death were all their lifetime subject to bondage."[3] From this passage it is shown with sufficient clearness that even the death of the body came about by the instigation and work of the devil,—in a word, from the sin which he persuaded man to commit ; nor is there any other reason why he should be said in strictness of truth to hold the power of death. Accordingly, He who died without any sin, original or actual, said in the passage I have already quoted : "Behold, the prince of this world," that is, the devil, who had the power of death, "cometh and findeth nothing in me,"—meaning, he shall find no sin in me, because of which he has caused men to die. As if the question were asked Him : Why then should you die? He says, "That all may know that I am doing the will of my Father, arise, let us go hence ;"[4] that is, that I may die, though I have no cause of death from sin under the author of sin, but only from obedience and righteousness, having become obedient unto death. Proof is likewise afforded us by this passage, that the fact of the faithful overcoming the fear of death is a part of the struggle of faith itself ; for all struggle would indeed be at an end, if immortality were at once to become the reward of them that believe.

CHAP. 52 [XXXII.] — WHY CHRIST, AFTER HIS RESURRECTION, WITHDREW HIS PRESENCE FROM THE WORLD.

Although, therefore, the Lord wrought many visible miracles in order that faith might sprout at first and be fed by infant nourishment, and grow to its full strength by and by out of this softness (for as faith becomes stronger the less does it seek such help) ; He nevertheless wished us to wait quietly, without visible inducements, for the promised hope, in order that "the just might live by faith ;"[5] and so great was this wish of His, that though He rose from the dead the third day, He did not desire to remain among men, but, after leaving a proof of his resurrection by showing Himself in the flesh to those whom He deigned to have for His witnesses of this event, He ascended into heaven, withdrawing Himself thus from their sight, and conferring no such thing on the flesh of any one of them as He had displayed in His own flesh, in order that they too "might live by faith," and in the present world might wait in patience and without visible inducements for the reward of that righteousness in which men live by faith, — a reward which should hereafter be visibly and openly bestowed. To this signification I believe that passage must be referred which He speaks concerning the Holy Ghost : "He will not come, unless I depart."[6] For this was in fact saying Ye shall not be able to live righteously by faith, which ye shall have as a gift of mine, — that is, from the Holy Ghost, — unless I withdraw from your eyes that which ye now gaze upon, in order that your heart may advance in spiritual growth by fixing its faith on invisible things. This righteousness of faith He constantly commends to them. Speaking of the Holy Ghost, He says, "He shall reprove the world of sin, and of righteousness, and of judgment : of sin, because they have not believed on me : of righteousness, because I go to the Father, and ye shall see me no more."[7] What is that righteousness, whereby men were not to see Him, except that "the just is to live by faith," and that we, not looking at the things which are seen, but at those which are not seen, are to wait in the Spirit for the hope of the righteousness that is by faith?

CHAP. 53 [XXXIII.] — AN OBJECTION OF THE PELAGIANS.

But those persons who say, "If the death of the body has happened by sin, we of course ought not to die after that remission of sins which the Redeemer has bestowed upon us," do not understand how it is that some things, whose guilt God has cancelled in order that they may not stand in our way after this life, He yet permits to remain for the contest of faith, in order that they may become the means of instructing and exercising those who are advancing in the

---

[1] Heb. xi. 13.
[2] Heb. xi. 39, 40.
[3] Heb. ii. 14.
[4] John xiv. 30, 31.

[5] Hab. ii. 4.
[6] John xvi. 7.
[7] John xvi. 8-10.

struggle after holiness. Might not some man, by not understanding this, raise a question and ask, If God has said to man because of his sin, "In the sweat of thy brow thou shalt eat thy bread: thorns also and thistles shall the ground bring forth to thee," [1] how comes it to pass that this labour and toil continues since the remission of sins, and that the ground of believers yields them this rough and terrible harvest? Again, since it was said to the woman in consequence of her sin, "In sorrow shalt thou bring forth children," [2] how is it that believing women, notwithstanding the remission of their sins, suffer the same pains in the process of parturition? And nevertheless it is an incontestable fact, that by reason of the sin which they had committed, the primeval man and woman heard these sentences pronounced by God, and deserved them; nor does any one resist these words of the sacred volume, which I have quoted about man's labour and woman's travail, unless some one who is utterly hostile to the catholic faith, and an adversary to the inspired writings.

CHAP. 54 [XXXIV.] — WHY PUNISHMENT IS STILL INFLICTED, AFTER SIN HAS BEEN FORGIVEN.

But, inasmuch as there are not wanting persons of such character, just as we say in answer to those who raise this question, that those things are punishments of sins before remission, which after remission become contests and exercises of the righteous; so again to such persons as are similarly perplexed about the death of the body, our answer ought to be so drawn as to show both that we acknowledge it to have accrued because of sin, and that we are not discouraged by the punishment of sins having been bequeathed to us for an exercise of discipline, in order that our great fear of it may be overcome by us as we advance in holiness. For if only small virtue accrued to "the faith which worketh by love" in conquering the fear of death, there would be no great glory for the martyrs; nor could the Lord say, "Greater love hath no man than this, that he lay down his life for his friends;" [3] which John in his epistle expresses in these terms: "As He laid down His life for us, so ought we to lay down our lives for the brethren." [4] In vain, therefore, would commendation be bestowed on the most eminent suffering in encountering or despising death for righteousness' sake, if there were not in death itself a really great and very severe trial. And the man who overcomes the fear of it by his faith, procures a great glory and just recompense for his faith itself. Wherefore it ought to surprise no one, either that the death of the body

could not possibly have happened to man unless sin had been previously committed, since it was of this that it was to become the punishment; nor that after the remission of their sins it comes to the faithful, in order that in their triumphing over the fear of it, the fortitude of righteousness may be exercised.

CHAP. 55. — TO RECOVER THE RIGHTEOUSNESS WHICH HAD BEEN LOST BY SIN, MAN HAS TO STRUGGLE, WITH ABUNDANT LABOUR AND SORROW.

The flesh which was originally created was not that sinful flesh in which man refused to maintain his righteousness amidst the delights of Paradise, wherefore God determined that sinful flesh should propagate itself after it had sinned, and struggle for the recovery of holiness, in many toils and troubles. Therefore, after Adam was driven out of Paradise, he had to dwell over against Eden, — that is, over against the garden of delights, — to indicate that it is by labours and sorrows, which are the very contraries of delights, that sinful flesh had to be educated, after it had failed amidst its first pleasures to maintain its holiness, previous to its becoming sinful flesh. As therefore our first parents, by their subsequent return to righteous living, by which they are supposed to have been released from the worst penalty of their sentence through the blood of the Lord, were still not deemed worthy to be recalled to Paradise during their life on earth, so in like manner our sinful flesh, even if a man lead a righteous life in it after the remission of his sins, does not deserve to be immediately exempted from that death which it has derived from its propagation of sin.[5]

CHAP. 56. — THE CASE OF DAVID, IN ILLUSTRATION.

Some such thought has occurred to us about the patriarch David, in the Book of Kings. After the prophet was sent to him, and threatened him with the evils which were to arise from the anger of God on account of the sin which he had committed, he obtained pardon by the confession of his sin, and the prophet replied that the shame and crime had been remitted to him; but yet, for all that, the evils with which God had threatened him followed in due course, so that he was brought low by his son. Now why is not an objection at once raised here: "If it was on account of his sin that God threatened him, why, when the sin was forgiven, did He fulfil His threat?" except because, if the cavil had been raised, it would have been most correctly answered, that the remission of the sin was given that the man

---

[1] Gen. iii. 18, 19.
[2] Gen. iii. 16.
[3] John xv. 13.
[4] 1 John iii. 16.

[5] See also his treatise, De Naturâ et Gratiâ, ch. xxiii.

might not be hindered from gaining the life eternal, but the threatened evil was still carried into effect, in order that the man's piety might be exercised and approved in the lowly condition to which he was reduced. Thus also God has both inflicted on man the death of his body, because of his sin, and, after his sins are forgiven, has not released him in order that he may be exercised in righteousness.

CHAP. 57 [XXXV.] — TURN TO NEITHER HAND.

Let us hold fast, then, the confession of this faith, without faltering or failure. One alone is there who was born without sin, in the likeness of sinful flesh, who lived without sin amid the sins of others, and who died without sin on account of our sins. "Let us turn neither to the right hand nor to the left."[1] For to turn to the right hand is to deceive oneself, by saying that we are without sin; and to turn to the left is to surrender oneself to one's sins with a sort of impunity, in I know not how perverse and depraved a recklessness. "God indeed knoweth the ways on the right hand,"[2] even He who alone is without sin, and is able to blot out our sins; "but the ways on the left hand are perverse,"[3] in friendship with sins. Of such inflexibility were those youths of twenty years,[4] who foretokened in figure God's new people; they entered the land of promise; they, it is said, turned neither to the right hand nor to the left.[5] Now this age of twenty is not to be compared with the age of children's innocence, but if I mistake not, this number is the shadow and echo of a mystery. For the Old Testament has its excellence in the five books of Moses, while the New Testament is most refulgent in the authority of the four Gospels. These numbers, when multiplied together, reach to the number twenty: four times five, or five times four, are twenty. Such a people (as I have already said), instructed in the kingdom of heaven by the two Testaments — the Old and the New — turning neither to the right hand, in a proud assumption of righteousness, nor to the left hand, in a reckless delight in sin, shall enter into the land of promise, where we shall have no longer either to pray that sins may be forgiven to us, or to fear that they may be punished in us, having been freed from them all by that Redeemer, who, not being "sold under sin,"[6] "hath redeemed Israel out of all his iniquities,"[7] whether committed in the actual life, or derived from the original transgression.

CHAP. 58 [XXXVI.] — "LIKENESS OF SINFUL FLESH" IMPLIES THE REALITY.

It is no small concession to the authority and truthfulness of the inspired pages which those persons have made, who, although unwilling to admit openly in their writings that remission of sins is necessary for infants, have yet confessed that they need redemption. Nothing that they have said differs indeed from another word, even that which is derived from Christian instruction. Whilst by those who faithfully read, faithfully hear, and faithfully hold fast the Holy Scriptures, it cannot be doubted that from that flesh, which first became sinful flesh by the choice of sin, and which has been subsequently transmitted to all through successive generations, there has been propagated a sinful flesh, with the single exception of that "likeness of sinful flesh,"[8] — which *likeness*, however, there could not have been, had there not been also the *reality* of sinful flesh.

CHAP. 59. — WHETHER THE SOUL IS PROPAGATED; ON OBSCURE POINTS, CONCERNING WHICH THE SCRIPTURES GIVE US NO ASSISTANCE, WE MUST BE ON OUR GUARD AGAINST FORMING HASTY JUDGMENTS AND OPINIONS; THE SCRIPTURES ARE CLEAR ENOUGH ON THOSE SUBJECTS WHICH ARE NECESSARY TO SALVATION.

Concerning *the soul*, indeed, the question arises, whether it, too, is propagated in the same way [as the flesh,] and bound by the same guilt, which is forgiven to it — for we cannot say that it is only the flesh of the infant, and not his soul also, which requires the help of a Saviour and Redeemer, or that the latter must not be included in that thanksgiving in the Psalms, where we read and repeat, "Bless the Lord, O my soul, and forget not all His benefits; who forgiveth all thine iniquities; who healeth all thy diseases; who redeemeth thy life from destruction."[9] Or if it be not likewise propagated, we may ask, whether, by the very fact of its being mingled with and weighed down by the sinful flesh, it still has need of the remission of its own sin, and of a redemption of its own, God being judge, in the height of His foreknowledge,[10] what infants do not deserve[11] to be absolved from that guilt, even before they are born, or have in any instance ever done anything good or evil. The question also arises, how God (even if He does not create souls by natural propagation) can yet not be the Author of that very guilt, on account of which redemption by the sacrament is necessary to the infant's soul. The subject is a wide and important one,[12]

---

[1] Prov. iv. 27.
[2] Same verse [in the Latin and Septuagint; the clause does not occur in the Hebrew].
[3] [See the last note.]
[4] Num. xiv. 29, 31.
[5] Josh. xxiii. 6, 8.
[6] Rom. vii. 14.
[7] Ps. xxv. 22.

[8] Rom. viii. 3.
[9] Ps. ciii. 2–4.
[10] We follow the reading, *per summam præscientiam*.
[11] Non mereantur.
[12] He treats it in his *Epistle*, 166; in his work, *De Animâ et ejus Origine;* and in his *De Libero Arbitrio*, 42.

and requires another treatise. The discussion, however, so far as I can judge, ought to be conducted with temper and moderation, so as to deserve the praise of cautious inquiry, rather than the censure of headstrong assertion. For whenever a question arises on an unusually obscure subject, on which no assistance can be rendered by clear and certain proofs of the Holy Scriptures, the presumption of man ought to restrain itself; nor should it attempt anything definite by leaning to either side. But if I must indeed be ignorant concerning any points of this sort, as to how they can be explained and proved, this much I should still believe, that from this very circumstance the Holy Scriptures would possess a most clear authority, whenever a point arose which no man could be ignorant of, without imperilling the salvation which has been promised him. You have now before you, [my dear Marcellinus,] this treatise, worked out to the best of my ability. I only wish that its value equalled its length; for its length I might probably be able to justify, only I should fear that, by adding the justification, I should stretch the prolixity beyond your endurance.

BOOK III.,

IN THE SHAPE OF A LETTER ADDRESSED TO THE SAME MARCELLINUS.

IN WHICH AUGUSTIN REFUTES SOME ERRORS OF PELAGIUS ON THE QUESTION OF THE MERITS OF SINS AND THE BAPTISM OF INFANTS — BEING SUNDRY ARGUMENTS OF HIS WHICH HE HAD INTERSPERSED AMONG HIS EXPOSITIONS OF SAINT PAUL, IN OPPOSITION TO ORIGINAL SIN.

To his beloved son Marcellinus, Augustin, bishop and servant of Christ and of the servants of Christ, sendeth greeting in the Lord.

CHAP. 1 [I.] — PELAGIUS ESTEEMED A HOLY MAN; HIS EXPOSITIONS ON SAINT PAUL.

THE questions which you proposed that I should write to you about, in opposition to those persons who say that Adam would have died even if he had not sinned, and that nothing of his sin has passed to his posterity by natural transmission; and especially on the subject of the baptism of infants, which the universal Church, with most pious and maternal care, maintains in constant celebration; and whether in this life there are, or have been, or ever will be, children of men without any sin at all — I have already discussed in two lengthy books. And I venture to think that if in them I have not met all the points which perplex all men's minds on such matters (an achievement which, I apprehend, — nay, which I have no doubt, — lies beyond the power either of myself, or of any other person), I have at all events prepared something in the shape of a firm ground on which those who defend the faith delivered to us by our fathers, against the novel opinions of its opponents, may at any time take their stand, not unarmed for the contest. However, within the last few days I have read some writings by Pelagius, — a holy man, as I am told, who has made no small progress in the Christian life, — containing some very brief expository notes on the epistles of the Apostle Paul; [1] and therein I found, on coming to the passage where the apostle says, "By one man sin entered into the world, and death by sin; and so it passed upon all men," [2] an argument which is used by those who say that infants

[1] [This commentary is also made known to us by Marius Merca-tor's *Commonitoria*, cap. 2, and has been preserved for us among the works of Jerome (Vallarsius' ed., tom. xi.), although probably not without alterations. It seems to have been composed before A.D. 410, at Rome. — W.]
[2] Rom. v. 12.

are not burdened with original sin. Now I confess that I have not refuted this argument in my lengthy treatise, because it did not indeed once occur to me that anybody was capable of thinking such sentiments. Being, however, unwilling to add to that work, which I had concluded, I have thought it right to insert in this epistle both the argument itself in the very words in which I read it, and the answer which it seems to me proper to give to it.

CHAP. 2 [II.] — PELAGIUS' OBJECTION; INFANTS RECKONED AMONG THE NUMBER OF BELIEVERS AND THE FAITHFUL.

In these terms, then, the argument is stated: — " But they who deny the transmission of sin endeavour to impugn it thus: If (say they) Adam's sin injured even those who do not sin, therefore Christ's righteousness also profits even those who do not believe; because 'In like manner, nay, much more,' he says, 'are men saved by one, than they had previously perished by one.'" Now to this argument, I repeat, I advanced no reply in the two books which I previously addressed to you; nor, indeed, had I proposed to myself such a task. But now I beg you first of all to observe, when they say, "If Adam's sin injures even those who do not sin, then Christ's righteousness also profits even those who do not believe," how absurd and false they judge it to be, that the righteousness of Christ should profit even those who do not believe; and that thence they think to put together such an argument as this: That no more could the first man's sin possibly do injury to infants who commit no sin, than the righteousness of Christ can benefit any who do not believe. Let them therefore tell us what is the benefit of Christ's righteousness to baptized infants; let them by all means tell us what they mean. For of course, since they do not forget that they are Christians themselves, they have no doubt that there is some benefit. But whatever be this benefit, it is incapable (as they themselves assert) of benefiting those who do not believe. Whence they are compelled to class baptized infants in the number of believers, and to assent to the authority of the Holy Universal Church, which does not account those unworthy of the name of believers, to whom the righteousness of Christ could be, according to them, of no use except as believers. As, therefore, by the answer of those, through whose agency they are born again, the Spirit of righteousness transfers to them that faith which, of their own will, they could not yet have; so the sinful flesh of those, through whose agency they are born, transfers to them that injury, which they have not yet contracted in their own life. And even as the Spirit of life regenerates them in Christ as believers, so also the body of death had generated them in Adam as sinners. The one generation is carnal, the other Spiritual; the one makes children of the flesh, the other children of the Spirit; the one children of death, the other children of the resurrection; the one the children of the world, the other the children of God; the one children of wrath, the other children of mercy; and thus the one binds them under original sin, the other liberates them from the bond of every sin.

CHAP. 3. — PELAGIUS MAKES GOD UNJUST.

We are driven at last to yield our assent on divine authority to that which we are unable to investigate with even the clearest intellect. It is well that they remind us themselves that Christ's righteousness is unable to profit any but believers, while they yet allow that it somewhat profits infants; according to this (as we have already said) they must, without evasion, find room for baptized infants among the number of believers. Consequently, if they are not baptized, they will have to rank amongst those who do not believe; and therefore they will not even have life, but "the wrath of God abideth on them," inasmuch as "he that believeth not the Son shall not see life; but the wrath of God abideth on him;"[1] and they are under judgment, since "he that believeth not is condemned already;"[2] and they shall be condemned, since "he that believeth, and is baptized, shall be saved; but he that believeth not shall be damned."[3] Let them, now, then see to it with what justice they can hold or strive to maintain that human beings have no part in eternal life, but in the wrath of God, and incur the divine judgment and condemnation, who are without sin; if, that is, as they cannot have any actual sin, so also they have within them no original sin.

CHAP. 4.

To the other points which Pelagius makes them urge who argue against original sin, I have already, I think, sufficiently and clearly replied in the two former books of my lengthy treatise. Now if my reply should seem to any persons to be brief or obscure, I beg their pardon, and request the favour of their coming to terms with those who perhaps censure my treatise, not for being too brief, but rather as being too long; whilst any who still do not understand the points which I cannot help thinking I have explained as clearly as the nature of the subject allowed me, shall certainly hear no blame or reproach from me for indifference, or want of understanding me.[4] I would rather that they should pray God to give them intelligence.

CHAP. 5 [III.] — PELAGIUS PRAISED BY SOME; ARGUMENTS AGAINST ORIGINAL SIN PROPOSED BY PELAGIUS IN HIS COMMENTARY.

But we must not indeed omit to observe that this good and praiseworthy man (as they who know him describe him to be) has not advanced this argument against the natural transmission of sin in his own person, but has reproduced what is alleged by those persons who disapprove of the doctrine, and this, not merely so far as I have just quoted and confuted the allegation, but also as to those other points on which I have now further undertaken to furnish a reply. Now, after saying, " If (they say) Adam's sin injured even those who do not sin, therefore Christ's righteousness also profits even those who do not believe," — which sentence, you will perceive from what I have said in answer to it, is not only not repugnant to what we hold, but even reminds us what we ought to hold, — he at once goes on to add, " Then they contend, if baptism cleanses away that old sin, those children who are born of two baptized parents must needs be free from this sin, for they could not have transmitted to their children what they did not possess themselves. Besides," says he, " if the soul is not of transmission, but only the flesh, then only the latter has the transmission of sin, and it alone deserves punishment; for they allege that it would be unjust for the soul, which is only now born, and comes not of the lump of Adam, to bear the burden of so old an alien sin. They say, likewise," says Pelagius, " that it cannot by any means be conceded that God, who remits to a man his own sins, should impute to him another's."

---

[1] John iii. 36.
[2] John iii. 18.
[3] Mark xvi. 16.

[4] [Or, " because they lack my own faculty of understanding the subject."]

CHAP. 6. — WHY PELAGIUS DOES NOT SPEAK IN
HIS OWN PERSON.

Pray, don't you see how Pelagius has inserted
the whole of this paragraph in his writings, not
in his own person, but in that of others, knowing so well the novelty of this unheard-of doctrine, which is now beginning to raise its voice
against the ancient ingrafted opinion of the
Church, that he was ashamed or afraid to
acknowledge it himself ?   And perhaps he does
not himself think that a man is born without sin
for whom he confesses that baptism to be necessary by which comes the remission of sins ; or
that the man is condemned without sin who
must be reckoned, when unbaptized, in the class
of non-believers, since the gospel of course cannot deceive us, when it most clearly asserts, " He
that believeth not shall be damned ; "[1] or, lastly,
that the image of God, when without sin, is not
admitted into the kingdom of God, forasmuch
as "except a man be born of water and of
the Spirit, he cannot enter into the kingdom
of God,"[2] — and so must either be precipitated
into eternal death without sin, or, what is still
more absurd, must have eternal life outside the
kingdom of God ; for the Lord, when foretelling
what He should say to His people at last, —
"Come, ye blessed of my Father, inherit the
kingdom prepared for you from the beginning
of the world,"[3] — also clearly indicated what
the kingdom was of which He was speaking, by
concluding thus : "So these shall go away into
everlasting punishment ; but the righteous into
life eternal."[4]   These opinions, then, and others
which spring from this central error, I believe so
worthy a man, and so good a Christian, does not
at all accept, as being too perverse and repugnant to Christian truth.   But it is quite possible
that he may, by the very arguments of those who
deny the transmission of sin, be still so far dis-
tressed as to be anxious to hear or know what
can be said in reply to them ; and on this
account he was both unwilling to keep silent the
tenets propounded by them who deny the transmission of sin, in order that he might get the
question in due time discussed, and, at the same
time, declined to report the opinions in his own
person, lest he should be supposed to entertain
them himself.

CHAP. 7 [IV.] — PROOF OF ORIGINAL SIN IN
INFANTS.

Now, although I may not be able myself to
refute the arguments of these men, I yet see
how necessary it is to adhere closely to the clearest statements of the Scriptures, in order that

the obscure passages may be explained by help
of these, or, if the mind be as yet unequal to
either perceiving them when explained, or inves-
tigating them whilst abstruse, let them be believed without misgiving.   But what can be
plainer than the many weighty testimonies of
the divine declarations, which afford to us the
clearest proof possible that without union with
Christ there is no man who can attain to eternal
life and salvation ; and that no man can unjustly
be damned, — that is, separated from that life
and salvation, — by the judgment of God ?   The
inevitable conclusion from these truths is this,
that, as nothing else is effected when infants are
baptized except that they are incorporated into
the church, in other words, that they are united
with the body and members of Christ, unless this
benefit has been bestowed upon them, they are
manifestly in danger of[5] damnation.   Damned,
however, they could not be if they really had
no sin.   Now, since their tender age could not
possibly have contracted sin in its own life, it
remains for us, even if we are as yet unable to
understand, at least to believe that infants inherit
original sin.

CHAP. 8. — JESUS IS THE SAVIOUR EVEN OF
INFANTS.

And therefore, if there is an ambiguity in the
apostle's words when he says, " By one man sin
entered into the world, and death by sin ; and
so it passed upon all men ; "[6] and if it is possible
for them to be drawn aside, and applied to some
other sense, — is there anything ambiguous in
this statement : " Except a man be born again
of water and of the Spirit, he cannot enter into
the kingdom of God ? "[2]   Is this, again, ambiguous : " Thou shalt call His name Jesus, for He
shall save His people from their sins ? "[7]   Is
there any doubt of what this means : " The
whole need not a physician, but they that are
sick ? "[8] — that is, Jesus is not needed by those
who have no sin, but by those who are to be
saved from sin.   Is there anything, again, ambiguous in this : " Except men eat the flesh of the
Son of man," that is, become partakers of His
body, " they shall not have life ? "[9]   By these
and similar statements, which I now pass over,
— absolutely clear in the light of God, and
absolutely certain by His authority, — does not
truth proclaim without ambiguity, that unbaptized infants not only cannot enter into the kingdom of God, but cannot have everlasting life,
except in the body of Christ, in order that they
may be incorporated into which they are washed

[1] Mark xvi. 16.
[2] John iii. 5.
[3] Matt. xxv. 34.
[4] Matt. xxv. 46.

[5] Pertinere ad.
[6] Rom. v. 12.
[7] Matt. i. 21.
[8] Matt. ix. 12.
[9] See John vi. 53.

in the sacrament of baptism? Does not truth, without any dubiety, testify that for no other reason are they carried by pious hands to Jesus (that is, to Christ, the Saviour and Physician), than that they may be healed of the plague of their sin by the medicine of His sacraments? Why then do we delay so to understand the apostle's very words, of which we perhaps used to have some doubt, that they may agree with these statements of which we can have no manner of doubt?

CHAP. 9. — THE AMBIGUITY OF "ADAM IS THE FIGURE OF HIM TO COME."

To me, however, no doubt presents itself about the whole of this passage, in which the apostle speaks of the condemnation of many through the sin of one, and the justification of many through the righteousness of One, except as to the words, "Adam is the figure of Him that was to come."[1] For this phrase in reality not only suits the sense which understands that Adam's posterity were to be born of the same form as himself along with sin, but the words are also capable of being drawn out into several distinct meanings. For we have ourselves perhaps actually contended for various senses from the words in question at different times,[2] and very likely we shall propound yet another view, which, however, will not be incompatible with the sense here mentioned; and even Pelagius has not always expounded the passage in one way. All the rest, however, of the passage in which these doubtful words occur, if its statements are carefully examined and treated, as I have tried my best to do in the first book of this treatise, will not (in spite of the obscurity of style necessarily engendered by the subject itself) fail to show the incompatibility of any other meaning than that which has secured the adhesion of the universal Church from the earliest times — that believing infants have obtained through the baptism of Christ the remission of original sin.

CHAP. 10 [V.] — HE SHOWS THAT CYPRIAN HAD NOT DOUBTED THE ORIGINAL SIN OF INFANTS.

Accordingly, it is not without reason that the blessed Cyprian[3] carefully shows how from the very first the Church has held this as a well understood article of faith. When he was asserting the fitness of infants only just born to receive Christ's baptism, on a certain occasion when he was consulted whether this ought to be administered before the eighth day, he endeavoured, as far as he could, to prove that they were per-

fect,[4] lest any one should suppose, from the number of the days (because it was on the eighth day that infants were before circumcised), that they so far lacked perfection. However, after bestowing upon them the full support of his argument, he still confessed that they were not free from original sin; because if he had denied this, he would have removed all reason for the very baptism which he was maintaining their fitness to receive. You can, if you wish, read for yourself the epistle of the illustrious martyr *On the Baptism of Little Children;* for it cannot fail to be within reach at Carthage. But I have deemed it right to transcribe some few statements of it into this letter of mine, so far as applies to the question before us; and I pray you to mark them carefully. "Now with respect," says he, "to the case of infants, whom you declared it would be improper to baptize if presented within the second and third day after their birth, since that due regard ought to be paid to the law of circumcision of old, so that you thought that the infant should not be baptized and sanctified before the eighth day after its birth, — a far different view has been formed of the question in our council. Not a man there assented to what you thought ought to be done; but the whole of us rather determined that to no one born of men ought God's mercy and grace to be denied. For since the Lord in His gospel says, 'The Son of man is not come to destroy men's lives, but to save them,'[5] so far as in us lies, not a soul ought, if possible, to be lost." You observe how in these words he supposes that it is fraught with ruin and death, not only to the flesh, but also to the soul, for one to depart this life without that saving sacrament. Wherefore, if he said nothing else, it was competent to us to conclude from his words that without sin the soul could not perish. See, however, what (when he shortly afterwards maintains the innocence of infants) he at the same time allows concerning them in the plainest terms: "But if," says he, "anything could hinder men from the attainment of grace, then their heavier sins might rather hinder those who have reached the stages of adults, and advanced life, and old age. Since, however, remission of sins is given even to the greatest sinners after they have believed, however much they have previously sinned against God, and since nobody is forbidden baptism and grace, how much more ought an infant not to be forbidden who newborn has done no sin, except that from having been born carnally after Adam he has contracted from his very birth the contagion of the primeval death! How, too, does this fact contribute in itself the more easily to their reception of the forgiveness of sins, that the remission which

---

[1] "*Adam formam futuri;*" see Rom. v. 14.
[2] Comp. *above,* Book i. c. 13; *Epist.* 157; *De Nuptiis,* ii. 44; and *Contra Julianum,* vi. 8.
[3] See Cyprian's *Epistle,* 64 (*ad Fidum*): also Augustin. *Epist.* 166; *De Nuptiis,* ii. 49; *Contra Julianum,* ii. 5; *Ad Bonifacium,* iv. 3; *Sermons,* 294.

[4] The word implies "of ripe age;" i.e., for "baptism."
[5] Luke ix. 56.

they have is not of their own sins, but of those of another!"

CHAP. 11.—THE ANCIENTS ASSUMED ORIGINAL SIN.

You see with what confidence this great man expresses himself after the ancient and undoubted rule of faith. In advancing such very certain statements, his object was by help of these firm conclusions to prove the uncertain point which had been submitted to him by his correspondent, and concerning which he informs him that a decree of a council had been passed, to the effect that, if an infant were brought even before the eighth day after his birth, no one should hesitate to baptize him. Now it was not then determined or confirmed by the council that infants were held bound by original sin as if it were new, or as if it were attacked by the opposition of some one; but when another controversy was being conducted, and the question was discussed, in reference to the law of the circumcision of the flesh, whether they ought to be baptized before the eighth day. None agreed with the person who denied this; because it was not an open question admitting of discussion, but was fixed and unassailable, that the soul would forfeit eternal salvation if it ended this life without obtaining the sacrament of baptism: but at the same time infants fresh from the womb were held to be affected only by the guilt of original sin. On this account, although remission of sins was easier in their case, because the sins were derived from another, it was nevertheless indispensable. It was on sure grounds like these that the uncertain question of the eighth day was solved, and the council decided that after a man was born, not a day ought to be lost in rendering him that succour which should prevent his perishing for ever. When also a reason was given for the circumcision of the flesh as being itself a shadow of what was to be, its purport was not that we should understand that baptism ought to be administered on the eighth day after birth, but rather that we are spiritually circumcised in the resurrection of Christ, who rose from the dead on the third day, indeed, after His passion, but among the days of the week, by which time is counted, on the eighth, that is, on the first day after the Sabbath.

CHAP. 12 [VI.] — THE UNIVERSAL CONSENSUS RESPECTING ORIGINAL SIN.

And now, again, with a strange boldness in new controversy, certain persons are endeavouring to make us uncertain on a point which our forefathers used to bring forward as most certainly fixed, whenever they would solve such questions as seemed uncertain to some. When this controversy, indeed, first began, I am unable to say; but one thing I know, that even the

holy Jerome, who is in our own day renowned for great industry and learning in ecclesiastical literature, for the solution of sundry questions treated in his writings, makes use of the same most certain assumption without exhibition of proofs. For instance, in his commentary on the prophet Jonah, when he comes to the passage where the infants were mentioned as chastened by the fast, he says:[1] "The greatest age comes first, and then all the rest is pervaded down to the least.[2] For there is no man without sin, whether the span of his age be but that of a single day, or he reckon many years to his life. For if the very stars are unclean in the sight of God,[3] how much more is a worm and corruption, such as are they who are held subject to the sin of the offending Adam?" If, indeed, we could readily interrogate this most learned man, how many authors who have treated of the divine Scriptures in both languages,[4] and have written on Christian controversies, would he mention to us, who have never held any other opinion since the Church of Christ was founded, — who neither received any other from their forefathers, nor handed down any other to their posterity? My own reading, indeed, has been far more limited, but yet I do not recollect ever having heard of any other doctrine on this point from Christians, who accept the two Testaments, whether established in the Catholic Church, or in any heretical or schismatic body whatever. I do not remember, I say, that I have at any time found any other doctrine in such writers as have contributed anything to literature of this kind, whether they have followed the canonical Scriptures, or have supposed that they have followed them, or had wished to be so supposed. From what quarter this question has suddenly come upon us I know not. A short time ago,[5] in a passing conversation with certain persons while we were at Carthage, my ears were suddenly offended with such a proposition as this: "That infants are not baptized for the purpose of receiving remission of sin, but that they may be sanctified in Christ." Although I was much disturbed by so novel an opinion, still, as there was no opportunity afforded me for gainsaying it, and as its propounders were not persons whose influence gave me anxiety, I readily let the subject slip into neglect and oblivion. And lo! it is now maintained with burning zeal against the Church; lo! it is committed to our permanent notice by writing; nay, the matter is brought to such a pitch of distracting influence, that we are even consulted on it by

---

[1] St. Jerome, on Jon. iii.
[2] Ver. 3.
[3] Job xxv. 4.
[4] Or "who have treated of both languages of the divine Scriptures."
[5] Probably in the year 411, when a conference was held at Carthage with the Donatists. Augustin says that he then saw Pelagius; see his work, *De Gestis Pelagii*, c. 46.

our brethren; and we are actually obliged to oppose its progress both by disputation and by writing.

CHAP. 13 [VII.] — THE ERROR OF JOVINIANUS DID NOT EXTEND SO FAR.

A few years ago there lived at Rome one Jovinian,[1] who is said to have persuaded nuns of even advanced age to marry, — not, indeed, by seduction, as if he wanted to make any of them his wife, but by contending that virgins who dedicated themselves to the ascetic life had no more merit before God than believing wives. It never entered his mind, however, along with this conceit, to venture to affirm that children of men are born without original sin. If, indeed, he had added such an opinion, the women might have more readily consented to marry, to give birth to such pure offspring. When this man's writings (for he dared to write) were by the brethren forwarded to Jerome to refute, he not only discovered no such error in them, but, while looking out his conceits for refutation, he found among other passages this very clear testimony to the doctrine of man's original sin, from which Jerome indeed felt satisfied of the man's belief of that doctrine.[2] These are his words when treating of it: "He who says that he abides in Christ, ought himself also to walk even as He walked.[3] We give our opponent the option to choose which alternative he likes. Does he abide in Christ, or does he not? If he does, then, let him walk like Christ. If, however, it is a rash thing to undertake to resemble the excellences of Christ, he abides not in Christ, because he walks not as Christ did. He did no sin, neither was any guile found in His mouth;[4] who, when He was reviled, reviled not again; and as a lamb before its shearer is dumb, so He opened not His mouth;[5] to whom the prince of this world came, and found nothing in Him;[6] whom, though He had done no sin, God made sin for us.[7] We, however, according to the Epistle of James, all commit many sins;[8] and none of us is pure from uncleanness, even if his life should be but of one day.[9] For who shall boast that he has a clean heart? Or who shall be confident that he is pure from sins? We are held guilty according to the likeness of Adam's transgression. Accordingly David also says: 'Behold,

[1] [This "Christian Epicurus," as he is called by the intemperate zeal of the asceticism of his day, was condemned as a heretic by councils at Rome and Milan in 390. According to Jerome, who wrote a book against him, he not only opposed asceticism, but also contended for the essential equality of all sins and of the punishments and rewards of the next world, and for the sinlessness of those baptized by the Spirit. — W.]
[2] See Jerome's work *Against Jovinian*, ii. near the beginning.
[3] John ii. 6.
[4] Isa. liii. 9.
[5] Isa. liii. 7.
[6] John xiv. 30.
[7] 2 Cor. v. 21.
[8] Jas iii. 2.
[9] Job xiv. 5.

I was shapen in iniquity; and in sin did my mother conceive me.'"[10]

CHAP. 14. — THE OPINIONS OF ALL CONTROVERSIALISTS WHATEVER ARE NOT, HOWEVER, CANONICAL AUTHORITY; ORIGINAL SIN, HOW ANOTHER'S; WE WERE ALL ONE MAN IN ADAM.

I have not quoted these words as if we might rely upon the opinions of every disputant as on canonical authority; but I have done it, that it may be seen how, from the beginning down to the present age, which has given birth to this novel opinion, the doctrine of original sin has been guarded with the utmost constancy as a part of the Church's faith, so that it is usually adduced as most certain ground whereon to refute other opinions when false, instead of being itself exposed to refutation by any one as false. Moreover, in the sacred books of the canon, the authority of this doctrine is vigorously asserted in the clearest and fullest way. The apostle exclaims: "By one man sin entered into the world, and death by sin; and so it passed upon all men, in which all have sinned."[11] Now from these words it cannot certainly be said, that Adam's sin has injured even those *who commit no sin*, for the Scripture says, "*In which all have sinned*." Nor, indeed, are those sins of infancy so said to be *another's*, as if they did not belong to the infants at all, inasmuch as all then sinned in Adam, when in his nature, by virtue of that innate power whereby he was able to produce them, they were all as yet the one Adam; but they are called *another's*,[12] because as yet they were not living their own lives, but the life of the one man contained whatsoever was in his future posterity.

CHAP. 15 [VIII.] — WE ALL SINNED ADAM'S SIN.

"It is," they say, "by no means conceded that God who remits to a man his own sins imputes to him another's." He remits, indeed, but it is to those regenerated by the Spirit, not to those generated by the flesh; but He imputes to a man no longer the sins of another, but only his own. They were no doubt the sins of another, whilst as yet they were not in existence who bore them when propagated; but now the sins belong to them by carnal generation, to whom they have not yet been remitted by spiritual regeneration.

CHAP. 16. — ORIGIN OF ERRORS; A SIMILE SOUGHT FROM THE FORESKIN OF THE CIRCUMCISED, AND FROM THE CHAFF OF WHEAT.

"But surely," say they, "if baptism cleanses the primeval sin, they who are born of two bap-

[10] Ps. li. 5.
[11] Rom. v. 12.
[12] Aliena.

tized parents ought to be free from this sin; for these could not have transmitted to their children that thing which they did not themselves possess." Now observe whence error usually thrives : it is when persons are able to start subjects which they are not able to understand. For before what audience, and in what words, can I explain how it is that sinful mortal beginnings bring no obstacle to those who have inaugurated other, immortal, beginnings, and at the same time prove an obstacle to those whom those very persons, against whom it was not an obstacle, have begotten out of the self-same sinful beginnings? How can a man understand these things, whose labouring mind is impeded both by its own prejudiced opinions and by the chain of its own stolid obstinacy? If indeed I had undertaken my cause in opposition to those who either altogether forbid the baptism of infants, or else contend that it is superfluous to baptize them, alleging that as they are born of believing parents, they must needs enjoy the merit of their parents; then it would have been my duty to have roused myself perhaps to greater labour and effort for the purpose of refuting their opinion. In that case, if I encountered a difficulty before obtuse and contentious men in refuting error and inculcating truth, owing to the obscurity which besets the nature of the subject, I should probably resort to such illustrations as were palpable and at hand ; and I should in my turn ask them some questions, — how, for instance, if they were puzzled to know in what way sin, after being cleansed by baptism, still remained in those who were begotten of baptized parents, they would explain how it is that the foreskin, after being removed by circumcision, should still remain in the sons of the circumcised? or again, how it happens that the chaff which is winnowed off so carefully by human labour still keeps its place in the grain which springs from the winnowed wheat?

CHAP. 17 [IX.] — CHRISTIANS DO NOT ALWAYS BE-GET CHRISTIAN, NOR THE PURE, PURE CHILDREN.

With these and such like palpable arguments, should I endeavour, as I best could, to convince those persons who believed that sacraments of cleansing were superfluously applied to the children of the cleansed, how right is the judgment of baptizing the infants of baptized parents, and how it may happen that to a man who has within him the twofold seed — of death in the flesh, and of immortality in the spirit — that may prove no obstacle, regenerated as he is by the Spirit, which is an obstacle to his son, who is generated by the flesh ; and that that may be cleansed in the one by remission, which in the other still requires cleansing by like remission, just as in the case supposed of circumcision, and as in the case of the winnowing and thrashing.

But now, when we are contending with those who allow that the children of the baptized ought to be baptized, we may much more conveniently conduct our discussion, and can say : You who assert that the children of such persons as have been cleansed from the pollution of sin ought to have been born without sin, why do you not perceive that by the same rule you might just as well say that the children of Christian parents ought to have been born Christians? Why, therefore, do you rather maintain that they ought to become Christians? Was there not in their parents, to whom it is said, "Know ye not that your bodies are the members of Christ?"[1] a Christian body? Perhaps you suppose that a Christian body may be born of Christian parents, without having received a Christian soul? Well, this would render the case much more wonderful still. For you would think of the soul one of two things as you pleased, — because, of course, you hold with the apostle, that before birth it had done nothing good or evil :[2] — either that it was derived by transmission, and just as the body of Christians is Christian, so should also their soul be Christian ; or else that it was created by Christ, either in the Christian body, or for the sake of the Christian body, and it ought therefore to have been created or given in a Christian condition. Unless perchance you shall pretend that, although Christian parents had it in their power to beget a Christian body, yet Christ Himself was not able to produce a Christian soul. Believe then the truth, and see that, as it has been possible (as you yourselves admit) for one who is not a Christian to be born of Christian parents, for one who is not a member of Christ to be born of members of Christ, and (that we may answer all, who, however falsely, are yet in some sense possessed with a sense of religion) for a man who is not consecrated to be born of parents who are consecrated ; so also it is quite possible for one who is not cleansed to be born of parents who are cleansed. Now what account will you give us, of why from Christian parents is born one who is not a Christian, unless it be that not generation, but regeneration makes Christians? Resolve therefore your own question with a like reason, that cleansing from sin comes to no one by being born, but to all by being born again. And thus any child who is born of parents who are cleansed, because born again, must himself be born again, in order that he too may be cleansed. For it has been quite possible for parents to transmit to their children that which they did not possess themselves, — thus resembling not only the wheat which yielded the chaff, and the circumcised the foreskin, but also the

---

[1] 1 Cor. vi. 15.
[2] Rom. ix. 11.

instance which you yourselves adduce, even that of believers who convey unbelief to their posterity; which, however, does not accrue to the faithful as regenerated by the Spirit, but it is owing to the fault of the mortal seed by which they have been born of the flesh. For in respect of the infants whom you judge it necessary to make believers by the sacrament of the faithful, you do not deny that they were born in unbelief, although of believing parents.

CHAP. 18 [X.] — IS THE SOUL DERIVED BY NATURAL PROPAGATION?

Well, but "if the soul is not propagated, but the flesh alone, then the latter alone has propagation of sin, and it alone deserves punishment:" this is what they think, saying "that it is unjust that the soul which is only recently produced, and that not out of Adam's substance, should bear the sin of another committed so long ago." Now observe, I pray you, how the circumspect Pelagius felt the question about the soul to be a very difficult one, and acted accordingly, — for the words which I have just quoted are copied from his book. He does not say absolutely, "Because the soul is not propagated," but hypothetically, *If the soul is not propagated,* rightly determining on so obscure a subject (on which we can find in Holy Scriptures no certain and obvious testimonies, or with very great difficulty discover any) to speak with hesitation rather than with confidence. Wherefore I too, on my side, answer this proposition with no hasty assertion: If the soul is not propagated, where is the justice that, what has been but recently created and is quite free from the contagion of sin, should be compelled in infants to endure the passions and other torments of the flesh, and, what is more terrible still, even the attacks of evil spirits? For never does the flesh so suffer anything of this kind that the living and feeling soul does not rather undergo the punishment. If this, indeed, is shown to be just, it may be shown, on the same terms, with what justice original sin comes to exist in our sinful flesh, to be subsequently cleansed by the sacrament of baptism and God's gracious mercy. If the former point cannot be shown, I imagine that the latter point is equally incapable of demonstration. We must therefore either bear with both positions in silence, and remember that we are human, or else we must prepare, at some other time, another work on the soul, if it shall appear necessary, discussing the whole question with caution and sobriety.

CHAP. 19 [XI.] — SIN AND DEATH IN ADAM, RIGHTEOUSNESS AND LIFE IN CHRIST.

What the apostle says: "By one man sin entered into the world, and death by sin; and so it passed upon all men, in which all have sinned;"[1] we must, however, for the present so accept as not to seem rashly and foolishly to oppose the many great passages of Holy Scripture, which teach us that no man can obtain eternal life without that union with Christ which is effected in Him and with Him, when we are imbued with His sacraments and incorporated with the members of His body. Now this statement which the apostle addresses to the Romans, "By one man sin entered into the world, and death by sin; and so it passed upon all men, in which all have sinned," tallies in sense with his words to the Corinthians: "Since by man came death, by Man came also the resurrection of the dead. For as in Adam all die, even so in Christ shall all be made alive."[2] For nobody doubts that the subject here referred to is the death of the body, because the apostle was with much earnestness dwelling on the resurrection of the body; and he seems to be silent here about sin for this reason, namely, because the question was not about righteousness. Both points are mentioned in the Epistle to the Romans, and both points are, at very great length, insisted on by the apostle, — sin in Adam, righteousness in Christ; and death in Adam, life in Christ. However, as I have observed already, I have thoroughly examined and opened, in the first book of this treatise, all these words of the apostle's argument, as far as I was able, and as much as seemed necessary.

CHAP. 20. — THE STING OF DEATH, WHAT?

But even in the passage to the Corinthians, where he had been treating fully of the resurrection, the apostle concludes his statement in such a way as not to permit us to doubt that the death of the body is the result of sin. For after he had said, "This corruptible must put on incorruption, and this mortal must put on immortality: so when this corruptible shall have put on incorruption, and this mortal immortality, then," he added, "shall be brought to pass the saying which is written, Death is swallowed up in victory. O death, where is thy victory? O death, where is thy sting?" and at last he subjoined these words: "The sting of death is sin; and the strength of sin is the law."[3] Now, because (as the apostle's words most plainly declare) death shall then be swallowed up in victory when this corruptible and mortal shall have put on incorruption and immortality, — that is, when "God shall quicken even our mortal bodies by His Spirit that dwelleth in us," — it manifestly follows that the sting of the body of this death, which is the contrary of the resur-

[1] Rom. v. 12.
[2] 1 Cor. xv. 21, 22.
[3] 1 Cor. xv. 53-56.

rection of the body, is sin. The sting, however, is that by which death was made, and not that which death made, since it is by sin that we die, and not by death that we sin. It is therefore called "the sting of death" on the principle which originated the phrase "the tree of life," — not because the life of man produced it, but because by it the life of man was made. In like manner "the tree of knowledge" was that whereby man's knowledge was made, not that which man made by his knowledge. So also "the sting of death" is that by which death was produced, not that which death made. We similarly use the expression "the cup of death," since by it some one has died, or might die, — not meaning, of course, a cup made by a dying or dead man.[1] The sting of death is therefore sin, because by the puncture of sin the human race has been slain. Why ask further: the death of what, — whether of the soul, or of the body? Whether the first which we are all of us now dying, or the second which the wicked hereafter shall die? There is no occasion for plying the question so curiously; there is no room for subterfuge. The words in which the apostle expresses the case answer the questions: "When this mortal," says he, "shall have put on immortality, then shall be brought to pass the saying which is written, Death is swallowed up in victory. O death, where is thy victory? O death, where is thy sting? The sting of death is sin, and the strength of sin is the law." He was treating of the resurrection of the body, wherein death shall be swallowed up in victory, when this mortal shall have put on immortality. Then over death itself shall be raised the shout of triumph, when at the resurrection of the body it shall be swallowed up in victory; then shall be said to it, "O death, where is thy victory? O death, where is thy sting?" To the death of the body, therefore, is this said. For victorious immortality shall swallow it up, when this mortal shall put on immortality. I repeat it, to the death of the body shall it be said, "Where is thy victory?" — that victory in which thou didst conquer all, so that even the Son of God engaged in conflict with thee, and by not shrinking but grappling with thee overcame. In these that die thou hast conquered; but thou art thyself conquered in these that rise again. Thy victory was but temporal, in which thou didst swallow up the bodies of them that die. Our victory will abide eternal, in which thou art swallowed up in the bodies of them that rise again. "Where is thy sting?" — that is, the sin wherewithal we are punctured and poisoned, so

that thou didst fix thyself in our very bodies, and for so long a time didst hold them in possession. "The sting of death is sin, and the strength of sin is the law." We all sinned in one, so that we all die in one; we received the law, not by amendment according to its precepts to put an end to sin, but by transgression to increase it. For "the law entered that sin might abound;"[2] and "the Scripture hath concluded all under sin;"[3] but "thanks be to God, who hath given us the victory through our Lord Jesus Christ,"[4] in order that "where sin abounded, grace might much more abound;"[2] and "that the promise by faith of Jesus Christ might be given to them that believe;"[3] and that we might overcome death by a deathless resurrection, and sin, "the sting" thereof, by a free justification.

CHAP. 21 [XII.] — THE PRECEPT ABOUT TOUCHING THE MENSTRUOUS WOMAN NOT TO BE FIGURATIVELY UNDERSTOOD; THE NECESSITY OF THE SACRAMENTS.

Let no one, then, on this subject be either deceived or a deceiver. The manifest sense of Holy Scripture which we have considered, removes all obscurities. Even as death is in this our mortal body derived from the beginning, so from the beginning has sin been drawn into this sinful flesh of ours, for the cure of which, both as it is derived by propagation and augmented by wilful transgression, as well as for the quickening of our flesh itself, our Physician came in the likeness of sinful flesh, who is not needed by the sound, but only by the sick, — and who came not to call the righteous, but sinners.[5] Therefore the saying of the apostle, when advising believers not to separate themselves from unbelieving partners: "For the unbelieving husband is sanctified by the wife, and the unbelieving wife is sanctified by the husband: else were your children unclean; but now are they holy,"[6] must be either so understood as both we ourselves elsewhere,[7] and as Pelagius in his notes on this same Epistle to the Corinthians,[8] has expounded it, according to the purport of the passages already mentioned, that sometimes wives gained husbands to Christ, and sometimes husbands converted wives, whilst the Christian will of even one of the parents prevailed towards making their children Christians; or else (as the apostle's words seem rather to indicate, and to a certain degree compel us) some particular sanctification is to be here understood, by which

---

[1] [This is only one of many examples of the care with which Augustin, writing for the popular eye, illustrates his exegetical points. "Of death" he thus shows is genitive of the object, not of the subject; giving to the phrase the meaning of "the sting which slays man." — W.]

[2] Rom. v. 20.
[3] Gal. iii. 22.
[4] 1 Cor. xv. 57.
[5] Mark ii. 17.
[6] 1 Cor. vii. 14.
[7] See Augustin's work *On the Sermon on the Mount*, i. 16.
[8] See the *Commentaries on St. Paul* in Jerome's works, vol. xi. (Vallarsius), the work of either Pelagius or one of his followers.

an unbelieving husband or wife was sanctified by the believing partner, and by which the children of the believing parents were sanctified, — whether it was that the husband or the wife, during the woman's menstruation, abstained from cohabiting, having learned that duty in the law (for Ezekiel classes this amongst the precepts which were not to be taken in a metaphorical sense[1]), or on account of some other voluntary sanctification which is not there expressly prescribed, — a sprinkling of holiness arising out of the close ties of married life and children. Nevertheless, whatever be the sanctification meant, this must be steadily held : that there is no other valid means of making Christians and remitting sins, except by men becoming believers through the sacrament according to the institution of Christ and the Church. For neither are unbelieving husbands and wives, notwithstanding their intimate union with holy and righteous spouses, cleansed of the sin which separates men from the kingdom of God and drives them into condemnation, nor are the children who are born of parents, however just and holy, absolved from the guilt of original sin, unless they have been baptized into Christ; and in behalf of these our plea should be the more earnest, the less able they are to urge one themselves.

CHAP. 22 [XIII.] — WE OUGHT TO BE ANXIOUS TO SECURE THE BAPTISM OF INFANTS.

For this is the point aimed at by the controversy, against the novelty of which we have to struggle by the aid of ancient truth : that it is clearly altogether superfluous for infants to be baptized. Not that this opinion is avowed in so many words, lest so firmly established a custom of the Church should be unable to endure its assailants. But if we are taught to render help to orphans, how much more ought we to labour in behalf of those children who, though under the protection of parents, will still be left more destitute and wretched than orphans,

should that grace of Christ be denied them, which they are all unable to demand for themselves?

CHAP. 23. — EPILOGUE.

As for what they say, that some men, by the use of their reason, have lived, and do live, in this world without sin, we should wish that it were true, we should strive to make it true, we should pray that it be true ; but, at the same time, we should confess that it is not yet true. For to those who wish and strive and worthily pray for this result, whatever sins remain in them are daily remitted because we sincerely pray, "Forgive us our debts, as we forgive our debtors."[2] Whosoever shall deny that this prayer is in this life necessary for every righteous man who knows and does the will of God, except the one Saint of saints, greatly errs, and is utterly incapable of pleasing Him whom he praises. Moreover, if he supposes himself to be such a character, "he deceives himself, and the truth is not in him,"[3] — for no other reason than that he thinks what is false. That Physician, then, who is not needed by the sound, but by the sick, knows how to heal us, and by healing to perfect us unto eternal life ; and He does not in this world take away death, although inflicted because of sin, from those whose sins He remits, in order that they may enter on their conflict, and overcome the fear of death with full sincerity of faith. In some cases, too, He declines to help even His righteous servants, so long as they are capable of still higher elevation, to the attainment of a perfect righteousness, in order that (while in His sight no man living is justified[4]) we may always feel it to be our duty to give Him thanks for mercifully bearing with us, and so, by holy humility, be healed of that first cause of all our failings, even the swellings of pride. This letter, as my intention first sketched it, was to have been a short one ; it has grown into a lengthy book. Would that it were as perfect as it has at last become complete !

---

[1] Ezek. xviii. 6.

[2] Matt. vi. 12.
[3] 1 John i. 8.
[4] Ps. cxliii. 2.

This is the end of this publication.

Any remaining blank pages are for our book binding requirements and are blank on purpose.

To search thousands of interesting publications like this one, please remember to visit our website at:

http://www.kessinger.net

CPSIA information can be obtained
at www.ICGtesting.com
Printed in the USA
LVHW021719091120
671186LV00009B/643